The Girls Who
Talked to Ghosts

The Fox family home in Hydesville, New York

by I.G. Edmonds

The Girls Who Talked to Ghosts

THE STORY OF KATIE AND MARGARETTA FOX

Holt, Rinehart and Winston • NEW YORK

Copyright © 1979 by I. G. Edmonds
All rights reserved, including the right to reproduce
this book or portions thereof in any form.
Published simultaneously in Canada by Holt, Rinehart
and Winston of Canada, Limited.
Printed in the United States of America

10 9 8 7 6 5 4 3 2 1

Library of Congress Cataloging in Publication Data
Edmonds, I. G.
     The girls who talked to ghosts.

     Bibliography: p. 153
     Includes index.
     SUMMARY: A biography, with emphasis on the early
years, of the Fox sisters, who claimed to communicate
with ghosts. Their experiences led to the founding of
the Spiritualist movement.
     1. Jencken, Catherine Fox, 1836–1892—Juvenile
literature. 2. Fox, Margaret, 1833–1893—Juvenile
literature. 3. Spiritualists—United States—Biography
—Juvenile literature. 4. Spiritualism—History—
Juvenile literature. [1. Jencken, Catherine Fox, 1836-
1892. 2. Fox, Margaret, 1833-1893. 3. Spiritualists]
I. Title.   BF1283.F7E35
133.9′1′0922 [920] [B] 78-14089   ISBN 0-03-042691-X

BT 6.95/4.29- 12/79

YA 133.91
Edmonds

Picture Sources

Frontis: The drawing of the Fox "spook house" is from an original
     in the Library of Congress.

Pages 26, 50, and 136: The portraits of Judge Edmonds and the
     Fox sisters are from Emma Hardinge's *Modern American
     Spiritualism* (1870).

Page 80: The drawing of the three sisters is a redrawn copy from
     an original Currier and Ives print made about 1850.

Page 131: The portrait of Margaretta is from *The Love-Life of
     Dr. Kane* (1866).

Contents

Introduction – About Ghosts

The belief in ghosts and spirits is very old. Some anthropologists—people who study the customs of mankind—believe that the idea of spirits came from the dreams of cavemen.

These primitive people had dreams but did not understand them. They knew that they did not leave their caves at night. Yet something inside them seemed to do so and had strange adventures. In time these cave people came to believe that this something inside them, which came and went in their dreams, did not die when their living bodies died. In this way the idea of spirits and ghosts was born.

We do not know if this theory is true. However, we do know that early man believed in spirits. This is proven by the way primitive people buried their dead, built altars, carved strange marks on rocks and cave walls, and modeled curious little statues.

Ghosts were thought to be fearful things. They appeared when they chose to do so. They frightened and often did harm to the living. There are thousands of stories of ghosts and haunted houses.

Then in March 1848 something happened that changed many ideas about ghosts and spirits. It began to seem to some people that ghosts, instead of being fearful things, might be friendly and eager to talk to the living.

If this is so, people asked, why had spirits never talked to the living before? Spiritualists—believers in the new ideas—had an answer to this question. Spirits have no bodies. Therefore, they lack power and strength. They can reach from spiritland to the land of the living only through the help of a living person. Not everyone, so the claim goes, can help spirits in this way. The person who can must be tuned—so to speak—to the spirit world. Such a person is called a *medium*—the medium through which spirits can converse with the living. Why did the spirits wait until 1848? The answer, Spiritualists claimed, is that spirits tried to contact the living before, but were misunderstood.

This claim that the dead are not really dead and are eager to help the living created a sensation. Many people were thrilled by the report. Others refused to believe it. Some, while believing, claimed it was antireligious and the sinister work of the devil.

Attacked from all sides, those who believed banded together to create what became known as Spiritualism. One of the most amazing things about Spiritualism is that it was all started by two young girls—Catharine (called Katie) and Margaretta (sometimes called Margaret or Maggie) Fox. They were the daughters of an upstate New York blacksmith named John Fox.

John Fox was German, and the original family name

was Voss. At one time he owned a large farm in Canada. He lost the land and began drinking. Then he deserted his family, but returned after several years. They moved to the United States, living in Rochester, New York, for a while, and then moved to Hydesville. The Foxes had a married son and daughter living on farms near Hydesville. Mrs. Fox wanted to be near them. Fox took a job as a blacksmith while trying to get enough money to go back to farming.

It was John and Margaret Fox's two youngest daughters who first talked with ghosts. It is not possible to tell exactly how old the two girls were at this time. Their mother gave different ages for them at different times. At first she tried to make them seem older. She said that Margaretta was fifteen, and that Katie, the younger of the two, was twelve. Later she said that Katie was seven and Margaretta nine on that fateful night when the ghost of a murdered man talked with them through raps.

From later statements of Margaretta, Horace Greeley, and others, it seems that Katie was eleven and a half and Margaretta thirteen.

The unusual story of the Fox sisters begins in Hydesville. As is fitting and proper for a tale about ghosts, their story begins in a haunted house. . . .

Strange Sounds in the Night

In December 1847 John Fox moved his family from Rochester, New York, to Hydesville, a town about twenty-five miles away. The family expected to have trouble finding a place to live. Then Arthur Hyde, son of the family for whom the town was named, sent word that he had an empty house to rent.

Mrs. Fox and the girls went to look at it. It was a box-shaped house. The bottom story was full height, but the second story was low roofed. Mrs. Fox was pleased with it.

"I did not expect to find such a nice place vacant," she said.

Arthur Hyde cleared his throat with embarrassment. He was a God-fearing man and would not lie. At the same time, he saw no reason for telling more than he should. The house was vacant because the old tenants had moved out, claiming that they could not sleep because ghosts made too much noise.

The Fox family moved in. In late February 1848, they also began to hear strange sounds in the night. Katie, the youngest daughter, complained to her mother about the odd rapping sounds.

"I think a ghost is after us!" she told Mrs. Fox.

"Nonsense!" her mother snapped. "The man next door is a shoemaker. The rapping you claim to hear is this man working at night."

Katie tried to argue. Mrs. Fox, busy with her work, refused to listen. Then a few days later Margaretta also complained about being awakened by noises in the night.

"And it shook our bed, too," she told her mother.

"And something *cold* touched my face!" Katie added.

Again Mrs. Fox refused to listen. "You are imagining things," she said. "Enough of this nonsense. Upstairs with you both. Clean up your room. It's a mess, as usual."

Then the strange noises became so loud that they awoke even Mr. and Mrs. Fox. The parents slept in the downstairs bedroom. The girls slept upstairs. John Fox thought the noises were made by a loose window rattling in the wind. He tightened the windows the next day. But that night they again heard the rapping sounds. The entire family got up and searched the house. They found nothing.

Mrs. Fox became so alarmed that she sent for her married son, David, who lived on a farm four miles away. Twenty-four-year-old David did not believe in ghosts. He told his mother that she was imagining things.

"But *I'm* not!" Katie cried. "I don't know how to imagine things like that. I heard it. And something cold touched my face!"

Margaretta, more quietly than her lively sister, also told David that she believed the house to be haunted.

David laughed at his sisters' fear. "Don't worry your pretty heads about a ghost," he told them. "Just tweak his nose like this and he'll run away."

He reached down and pulled Katie's nose. She jerked back, crying, "Stop that! You'll make me have a long nose!"

The family heard no noises for the next several days. Then on the night of March 30, 1848, the strange sounds returned. They were louder than before. Later Mrs. Fox wrote about this night in a signed statement collected by a writer:

> On March 30 we were disturbed all night. The noises sounded in all parts of the house. My husband stood on one side of the door. I stood on the other. And the knocks were heard on the door between us.
>
> Then we heard footsteps in the pantry and walking downstairs. We could not rest. I thought the house must be haunted by some unhappy spirit. I had often heard of such things.

The family got little sleep that night. Katie and Margaretta were afraid to sleep upstairs. John Fox moved their bed down into his and Margaret's bedroom. The next night (March 31) the family went to bed early. Mrs. Fox told the girls to pay no attention if the sounds started again.

She unpinned her long hair and put it in loose braids for the night. She got wearily into bed while John Fox banked the fire in the heating stove.

Suddenly the odd rapping sounds began again. "I know it is those windows," John Fox said angrily to his wife. "Listen while I shake them."

Katie and Margaretta sat up in bed. They pulled the quilts up around their necks. The weather was still cold and the fire in the heater was banked. They watched fearfully as John Fox strode across the room and shook the window in its frame. It made a rattling noise.

"Does that sound like the ghostly raps?" he asked.

"Not much," Mrs. Fox replied. "The ghostly raps have a more hollow sound."

Then raps suddenly sounded across the room from the window.

"Hear that?" she said, her voice shaking. "It is not the same, John."

John Fox was not ready to admit that there was really a ghost in his house. "Maybe the second noises are echoes. That is why they sound different. Now all of you listen while I shake the window again."

He shook the window in its frame. Raps again sounded from the other side of the room. But they came from a different place than before. John Fox shook the window again. The strange rapping was heard from still a different part of the room. Also, the time between the noises made by the window and the raps that followed was too long for the raps to be echoes.

John Fox looked at his wife with a baffled expression on his face.

"There is nothing we can do, John," Mrs. Fox said wearily. "Blow out the candle and come to bed. We will have to find another place to live. We cannot keep on putting up with this."

Suddenly Katie cried, "Mama! The sounds seem to *answer* Daddy! They made the same number of raps as the window."

"You are imagining things, child," Mrs. Fox said.

But Katie was not to be put off. "Mr. Splitfoot!" she cried in a loud voice, meaning the Devil. "Do as I do!"

She clapped her hands four times. Immediately there were four answering raps from across the room.

"See, Mama!" Katie cried. "It answered me! It—*oh*!"

She suddenly realized that the strange rapper had really answered her. This frightened her so badly that she ducked her head under the quilts. She snuggled up close against Margaretta, throwing her arms about her sister. Margaretta was a much quieter child than her lively little sister. She said nothing, but her eyes were very large as she stared about the room. The light from the single candle, sitting on the dresser near her parents' bed, caused deep mysterious shadows all through the room.

For a long moment none of the family said anything. Then Mrs. Fox said in a shaky voice, "It was just an accident. Nothing answered you, dear."

"Let me try," Margaretta said in a small, quiet voice. "Do as I do. Count to four."

She clapped her hands four times, pausing for a second between each clap. For a breathless moment there was no answering sound. Then from the direction of the dresser four raps sounded. They were spaced out exactly as Margaretta had spaced hers.

Mrs. Fox had gotten out of bed. Now she slowly sat down on the edge of the bed. "John," she whispered in a choked voice. "What is this?"

John Fox just stared at his wife, unable to speak. His tough blacksmith's hands gripped the back of a cane-bottom chair as if he was going to use it for protection.

Katie broke the stunned silence. "Mama!" she cried. "I know what it is! Tomorrow is April Fool's Day. Someone is trying to fool us."

"But this has been going on for weeks," Mrs. Fox replied. She took a deep breath.

"Also, we have searched the house," John Fox added. "There is no one here."

Mrs. Fox took a deep breath. "If this—what-ever-it-is —really answered Katie and Maggie, then maybe it will answer me. Let me try something."

Then to the invisible knocker she said, "Answer my questions with your knocks. First, count to ten."

There was a brief pause. Then the rappings began. The tense family counted. While others counted silently, Katie called the numbers aloud. The rappings stopped at ten.

Mrs. Fox's voice trembled as she asked her next question. "How old is my daughter Margaretta?"

She was answered by twelve knocks. Mrs. Fox looked helplessly at her husband. John Fox stared back at her silently. Margaretta just sat up in bed, the quilt pulled up under her chin. But Katie giggled. "See!" she said. "I was right. It does answer back!"

Then Mrs. Fox asked Katie's age. She got the right answer. She asked how many children she had. There were seven knocks.

"That's wrong!" she whispered.

The seven knocks repeated themselves.

"What about the baby?" Katie asked.

Mrs. Fox sucked in her breath. "How many *living* children do we have?" she asked.

There were six knocks this time. This was correct. In

addition to Katie and Margaretta at home, the Foxes had a married son and daughter in Hydesville, another married daughter in Canada, and a widowed daughter living in Rochester, New York.

"The little one," Mrs. Fox asked. "When did he die? At what age?"

There were three raps.

Mrs. Fox was so pale that her husband said anxiously, "You had better stop now."

"No," she said. "I must *know*."

To the invisible rapper she said, "Are you human? Let two raps mean yes."

There were no answering knocks. Mrs. Fox then said, "A-are you a spirit or ghost?"

There were two answering raps, meaning yes.

John Fox, his own face as pale as his wife's, again asked her to stop. She refused and went on with her questions.

Slowly, asking questions that could be answered yes or no, Mrs. Fox got the story of the mysterious rapper. He claimed to be a thirty-one-year-old man who had been murdered in this house. He had come as a peddler and had been killed for his money. He said his body was buried in the cellar.

"No one will ever believe this," John Fox said in a strained voice.

"Will you answer questions for our neighbors?" Mrs. Fox asked.

There were two answering raps, meaning yes.

Margaret Fox said to her husband. "John, go get Mrs. Redfield!"

John Fox hurried next door to get their neighbor. Mrs.

Redfield was a large, no-nonsense type of woman. She was known for her sharp tongue. She always said exactly what she thought. She listened in astonishment to John Fox's claim that his family was talking to a ghost.

"Ridiculous!" she snapped. "Those mischievous children of yours are just playing a prank on their mother. I'll show you."

Mrs. Redfield followed Fox back to the haunted house. Her manner changed when she saw how frightened Mrs. Fox was, but she still looked suspiciously at Katie and Margaretta.

Then Mrs. Fox asked some questions of the ghost. These were answered correctly. Next Mrs. Fox asked Mrs. Redfield to put her own questions to the ghost. When these were correctly answered, Mrs. Redfield nervously sat down on the edge of the Foxes' bed. For once in her life, Mrs. Redfield was speechless.

"The ghost talked to *me* first!" Katie put in proudly.

Her mother hushed her. Mrs. Redfield got up shakily. "I must get my husband," she said.

She left and returned shortly with Charles Redfield, a shoemaker. Redfield listened, asked his own questions, and then hurried off to bring more neighbors. Among those who came were Artemus Hyde, son of the man who owned the haunted house, and William Duesler.

Duesler later wrote an account of what he saw and heard that fateful night. He said that the house was soon filled with people. They kept asking the same questions over and over, and getting the same replies about the ghost's body having been buried in the cellar.

Margaretta fell asleep during the questioning, but Katie remained wide awake to the end. The visitors began leaving at midnight. They left talking excitedly among themselves about the strange things they had heard.

Mrs. Redfield insisted that Mrs. Fox and the girls go home with her.

"You don't have enough room——" Mrs. Fox began.

"Charlie can stay here with John to see if anything else happens," Mrs. Redfield replied.

Mr. Redfield looked startled, but he did not argue with his wife. He agreed to keep John Fox company in the haunted house. Margaretta was awakened. As the two girls walked with their mother and Mrs. Redfield to the neighboring house, Katie said, "I am not afraid. If the ghost was not our friend, he would not have talked to us."

"Perhaps," Mrs. Redfield replied. "But I just can't trust *ghosts.*"

·2·

The Haunted House

The next day was Saturday. When Mrs. Fox and the girls returned soon after sunup, there was already a crowd at the house. The front room was crowded and many stood outside waiting for a chance to come in.

The peddler's ghost made no sound during the day. Consequently, many people believed that the so-called knockings were just imagination. This caused some hot arguments.

"Whoever heard of a ghost in the daytime?" Charlie Redfield asked angrily. "Ghosts are only heard at night."

Then William Duesler got up on a chair so all could see and hear him. He told the newcomers exactly what he had seen and heard the night before.

"I laughed when Mrs. Redfield came and told us that the Fox family was talking to a ghost," he said. "I told her I would soon prove that it was all a hoax. Well, I did not do so."

The rapping started again when it grew dark. Some suspicious people watched Katie and Margaretta closely.

They saw nothing to indicate that the girls were making the noises.

At this point someone recalled that the Weekman family, who lived in the house before the Foxes, complained of night noises. Here again, a child was involved. One woman recalled that Mrs. Weekman told her that they heard both knocks and the sound of someone walking in the house. When they searched the place, they found no one.

Then there was an incident involving the Weekmans' daughter that was very much like what had happened to Katie Fox. According to a statement made later, Mrs. Weekman said, "One of our little girls woke us all up by screaming very loud. She slept in the bedroom where the noises are now heard. [She meant the room where the Fox family heard the raps.] My husband and I, and our hired girl, got up to see what was the matter. Our little girl sat up in bed, crying and screaming. It was some time before we could find out what the matter was.

"Then she said that something had been moving about, over her head and face—that it was cold, and she did not know what it was. She was very much frightened. This was between twelve and one o'clock at night. She got up and got into bed with us, but it was a long time before she could go to sleep. She was eight years old at the time."

There were those who thought that the Weekman girl only had a nightmare. But others recalled that Michael Weekman, the father, told of mysterious knockings in the house. This was almost exactly like the time Margaret and John Fox thought someone was rapping on their door.

Later Mr. Weekman was asked to write down what had happened to him. Investigators wanted to compare his story with that of John Fox. This is what Weekman wrote:

We used to live in the house now occupied by Mr. Fox, in which they say strange noises are heard. We lived there for a year and a half.

One evening about bedtime I heard the rapping. I supposed it was someone knocking at the door. I went to the door. I did not find anyone there. I went back. Just as I was getting into bed I heard the rapping again. I opened the door quickly, but could see no one there.

I went and got into bed. I thought someone was making game of me. After a few minutes I heard the knocking again. After waiting a few minutes and still hearing the noises, I got up and went to the door. This time I went clear outside and looked around the house. I could find no one.

I went back inside and shut the door. I held on to the latch. I thought if there was someone there I would catch them. In a minute or two I heard the rappings again. My hand was on the door, and the knockings appeared to be on the door. I opened it and sprang out. But there was no one in sight. I went around the house again, but could find no one, as before.

My wife told me I had better not go out of doors again. It might be that someone wanted to hurt me. I did not know what to think of all this. It seemed so strange.

The visitors to the Fox home thought about this when, in the evening, the raps started again. They noted that the raps did not sound unless Katie or Margaretta was near. Years later a man who, as a boy, was at the Fox house that night said he suspected that Katie was making the sounds. He knew her from school and knew how fun-loving she was. He watched her closely. She seemed much quieter than usual, but he could see nothing to show that she had anything to do with the mysterious rappings.

He watched her while William Duesler was questioning the ghost. She sat quietly with her hands folded in her lap. She did not move. After Duesler, several others who had not been there the previous night asked questions. They had the ghost retell his story of being murdered and buried in the cellar.

After that, a group of men went down to the cellar. They heard rapping noises as they went down the stairs. One of the men was sent back upstairs to see if anyone was beating on the floor above. He found nothing to account for the raps.

Then one man went around the cellar, sticking a crowbar in the earthen floor. Each time he would ask, "Is it here?" Finally, after several tries, there were answering raps from the spirit.

Later one of the men said, "The raps did not seem to come from the bedroom overhead. As I swung my lantern around, I spied one of the Fox girls [Katie] sitting at the head of the stairway leading down to the cellar from inside the house."

He thought it was she who was making the noises, but admitted that the raps did not seem to come from her direction. It was getting late and they decided against digging that night.

The next day was Sunday, April 2. Again the house was crowded with curious visitors. For the first time the raps were heard in the daytime. Mrs. Fox guided those visitors who wanted to ask questions of the rapping ghost. These answers came only if either Katie or Margaretta was present.

David Fox still refused to believe that a spirit was making the raps. He told Mrs. Fox so. Katie interrupted to ask what he thought made them.

"Maybe it is *you!*" her brother replied.

Katie giggled. "I could fool Mama maybe, but I could never fool *you*," she said, laughing.

"Nor could you fool me," William Duesler said. "But like David I do not believe in ghosts. And I'll not believe in them, especially this one, until I see his bones dug up from the cellar."

"That we should soon know about," David replied. "We are going to start digging as soon as Steve Smith gets here."

Smith, a son-in-law of the Fox family, had helped locate the spot where the body was supposed to be buried. After Smith arrived, John and David Fox, William Duesler, and another neighbor, Carlos Hyde, joined him in the cellar. They began digging at the spot indicated by the ghostly rappings the night before. They had dug only three feet when water began to fill the hole. The Hyde house was located on low ground near a stream. They tried to bail the water out, but it came back faster than they could remove it.

On Monday they tried again. David brought in a hand pump, but they could not keep the water from seeping into the hole. Duesler said it would be July before the ground was dry enough for them to dig successfully.

By this time Margaret Fox was almost a nervous wreck. She said she would not stay in the Hyde house a day longer. John Fox then borrowed a wagon and drove her and the two girls to David Fox's farm four miles from town.

They soon learned that they had not left the ghost behind. Raps now sounded in David Fox's home. Mrs. Fox was determined to have nothing more to do with the rapper. She threatened to spank Katie and Margaretta if they spoke to the ghost.

Still the unhappy spirit went *rap, rap, rap!* Mrs. Fox would sit tight-lipped, looking at her daughters. The expression on her worn face dared either to make a sound.

In the meantime, the story of the Hydesville ghost was picked up by local newspapers. Most editors treated it as a joke. Some declared it a hoax.

The story was carried by Rochester newspapers. For some reason, Leah Fox Fish, the Foxes' oldest daughter, did not see the story, although she lived in Rochester.

Mrs. Fish had married when she was fourteen. Her husband deserted her soon after their daughter, Elizabeth, was born. Mrs. Fish then became a piano teacher to support herself and her child. One of her students told her about the stories of the knocking ghost of Hydesville.

Leah Fish was angry because none of her family had written to her about their ghost. It was May 7 when she first heard of it. Five weeks had passed since Katie had clapped her hands and received an answering number of claps from the spirit.

Leah was then thirty-four years old. She had grown into a determined woman who liked to have her way about

Leah Fox Fish, oldest of the Fox daughters.

everything. In addition, she was bitter about her hard life. She did not make much money teaching and was barely able to live on what she made. It struck her that money might be made from her family's talking ghost. From what she had heard, the ghost would rap out his messages only in the presence of either Katie or Margaretta. It seemed to Leah that someone should pay for the girls' services.

Leah sent word to her students that she would be gone

for a few days. Then she took a canal boat for Newark. There she hired a buggy and drove on to Hydesville. She found the ghost house closed. So she talked to Mrs. Redfield, who tried to show her the bedroom where the rappings occurred. However, Hyde had locked the house when the Fox family moved out. Leah looked in the window and then drove to David's farm, where Mrs. Fox and the girls were staying. John Fox remained in Hydesville to be near his work.

Leah was shocked at the sight of her mother. Mrs. Fox's hair had turned white. She looked tired and old. She had become very nervous and twisted her hands as she talked. She truly believed that she and the girls had actually talked with a ghost.

Leah had long serious talks with her mother and sisters. Later she talked with David about digging up the bones the ghost claimed were buried in the cellar. David said angrily that he did not believe in ghosts.

"I'll have nothing more to do with this mess," he said.

"If it is not a ghost, then who or what is making these raps?" Leah asked. "You heard them, didn't you?"

"I heard them," David said shortly. "But I don't want to talk about it anymore. It has caused us nothing but trouble. And no good will ever come of fooling with spirits. When people die, they should stay dead."

The rappings had followed the girls to David's home and Leah was eager to hear them herself. The first night she was disappointed. The ghost made no noise. The second night there were rappings. Leah was entranced.

"Ask it a question!" she whispered.

"I'll have nothing more to do with it," Mrs. Fox replied.

"Will you ask it a question, Katie?" Leah appealed to her sister.

"You ask," Katie said. "It's really nice. It will answer you."

Leah Fox hesitated. Then in a trembling voice she asked, "What is my daughter's name?"

There were five answering raps. Leah looked inquiringly at Katie. "E is the fifth letter of the alphabet," the younger girl replied.

The unseen rapper then gave twelve raps, and after another pause nine more. This added up to E-L-I—. Then there was silence and they lost contact. The first three letters were enough to convince Leah.

Later, after their mother went to bed, Leah went upstairs and had a long talk with Katie and Margaretta. The next morning Leah said she had to return to her music students if she expected to keep them. Then she asked if Katie could go back to Rochester with her.

Mrs. Fox was surprised. Leah had not shown much interest in her younger sisters when they all lived in Rochester.

"You said that the ghost raps only when the girls are close by," Leah said to her mother. "Perhaps if we separate them, it will go away. I can take Katie back with me. Then we can see what happens."

Mrs. Fox agreed. She was thoroughly sick of the continued nightly noise. Katie was delighted. Margaretta pouted because she could not go. Leah explained that they wanted to see what would happen if the girls were separated. Later Margaretta and Mrs. Fox could join them.

Katie and Leah set out the next morning by buggy for Newark. There they took a canal boat to Rochester. The boat, pulled by horses along the Erie Canal, moved slowly along. Leah and Katie were sitting on deck watching the countryside slide past when raps sounded on the deck near their feet.

In a book she wrote years later, Leah said she was dismayed to find that the raps had followed them. However, this does not seem to have been true. She was actually pleased, for she intended to use the ghostly rappings to make money. Katie, of course, was delighted.

"This shows he likes me better than the others," she said proudly. "He followed me instead of staying with them!"

·3·

The First Seances

Leah claimed later that the ghost forced itself upon them. This is not true, as a bitter Margaretta would someday reveal. Leah saw in the ghost talk a way to make large sums of money.

She immediately invited some of her friends to hear the rappings. Katie was delighted to preside at these first séances. Actually the ghostly meetings were at first called "sittings." Later someone fancied up the word by calling it "séance," which is a French word that means sitting. It now means a meeting in which people try to contact spirits.

Leah's friends brought in others who wanted to ask questions of the friendly spirit. But as word of this got around, Leah's neighbors complained. Finally she was forced to move to a different street. The minister of her church heard about the spirit sittings. He claimed that they were the work of the devil, and ordered Leah to stop conducting them in her house. She angrily refused to stop the séances. She was dropped from the church's membership.

Ministers from three other churches called at different times. They thought the ghost was real, but from the devil. They offered to exorcise it. Leah was dismayed. She did not want the ghost banished, but feared that it would look bad if she refused.

Katie saved the day for her. "Let them come," she told Leah. "They can only drive away bad spirits. Our spirit is a very good one. He will not go away, no matter what they say to him."

Leah was relieved and let them come. It proved out as Katie claimed it would. The ministers' attempts to exorcise Katie's ghost—at least she called him hers—were not successful. Leah breathed easier. She used this in her arguments that Katie's séances did not violate religious beliefs.

Leah's neighbors were not convinced. They said the Foxes were wicked people. They stopped sending their children for piano lessons. Leah did not care. She started charging people to ask questions—through Katie's mediumship—of the ghost. Shortly after this, Mrs. Fox and Margaretta joined them. Margaretta also began charging for séances. Years later Margaretta said she and Katie got none of the money. Leah kept it all.

This was the beginning of the famous "rapping" séances. Katie originated the idea when she first asked the ghost to answer her. Leah turned it into a popular business. Next to these two, the persons who did most to spread Spiritualism in the beginning were two friends of Leah's. They were Isaac Post and E. W. Capron. Post and his wife, members of the Quaker faith, were the first friends Leah called in to hear Katie rap with the spirit. Capron was a young businessman who lived in Auburn, New York. He had been in Rochester on business when his friend Post invited him to go to the Fish house to hear the ghost talk.

Later Capron wrote a book about the beginning of Spiritualism. He included in the book letters he had asked friends to write about what they saw and heard in these first séances. One of the most remarkable was written by George Willets.

Willets was visiting in Rochester from his home near Buffalo. He was staying with Isaac Post. Post told Willets about the mysterious rappings that happened in the presence of the Fox girl. Willets said he found it impossible to believe that a spirit could communicate in this manner. But he agreed to go to a séance.

At this time Willets was having trouble finding work. He had decided to move his family to Michigan and clear land for a farm.

At the Fish home he met Leah, Margaretta, and Mrs. Fox. By this time—late summer 1848—the money the girls were making from the séances had overcome Mrs. Fox's horror of the ghost. Katie was visiting next door and Mrs. Fox sent for her. She arrived out of breath and joined Margaretta in a séance trance. Willets was not introduced to the Foxes by name. Only Isaac and Amy Post knew who he was.

Knocks were immediately heard all about the room. First one and then the other girl gave Willets messages from the spirits. These spirits, the girls said, were dead members of Willets' family.

First, Margaretta said that Willets' father did not want him to move to Michigan. This surprised Willets, for no one knew he intended to move. There were more raps. Katie said that Willets' mother also opposed the move. Then there were soft raps near Willets' chair. Katie said it was Willets' dead baby sister.

A single candle burned in the room. A breeze from the window fluttered the flame. This caused trembling shadows to move in the room. Willets felt a chill. He did not believe ghosts were talking to him. Yet the raps made him uneasy. He could not understand how the girls could possibly have known that he was planning to move to Michigan. Even Isaac Post did not know it. Willets said that large drops of perspiration streaked down his face as the séance continued.

Willets wrote: "I gathered courage. I thought I would dispel the illusion. I said, 'As you seem to know my father and his mind concerning me, perhaps you can tell me his name.' "

Willets said that Leah and the two younger girls sat quietly looking at him. Then he heard raps coming from the center of the table. He quickly looked under the table to see what was causing the sounds. He saw nothing. The noises continued for some time and were divided by brief pauses. Each set of raps spelled out a letter of the alphabet. Katie Fox spoke each letter as it was completed. The letters spelled out the name "William Willets."

"I was never so astonished in my whole life," Willets wrote.

He was even more astonished when the ghost spelled out another message, asking for Willets, Post, and the "little girl" [Katie] to withdraw into another room.

Willets then had a three-hour interview with what seemed to be the ghost of his father. There was no other person in the room except himself, Post, and Katie. Willets listened in amazement as the ghost rapped out messages. The ghost said that he had died seven years before. This was true, Willets admitted. His father had died in

1841, and he was sure that no one there knew this but himself. The ghost said that Willets should not go to Michigan because his health was too poor to clear land to make a farm. The ghost advised his son to buy a farm outside Rochester. He said that George could get a farm there for about $150 an acre.

The ghost spelled out the name of the owner of the land. Then slowly, rap by rap, the knockings formed these words, "Thee will not meet this man before ten o'clock. But thee may seek him earlier."

Willets still intended to move to Michigan, but he wanted to check on what the girls had told him. He found there was a man with land to sell as they claimed the ghost said. Since the alleged ghost of his father said he could not see this man before ten o'clock, Willets deliberately went to see him at seven o'clock. The man was gone, but his wife said he would return at noon.

Willets still did not believe he had received a ghostly message from his father. But he wanted to see the land anyway. He searched for the landowner for some time and finally found him.

"After talking with him five or six minutes, I thought of looking at my watch," Willets wrote. "*It was seven minutes past ten!*" Then when Willets asked about the land, "the owner said he had 50 acres and would sell it all or any part of it for $150 an acre. I went home and pondered these strange things."

He continued to ponder for three months. Then he moved to Rochester.

"A few days after getting to Rochester," Willets said, "the little girl spoken of [that is, Katie Fox] came round to our house. She said the spirit had directed her to come. She did not know why."

Willets asked the spirit why he had sent Katie. He got this reply through raps on the door, walls, and ceiling: "I told thee if thee would come to Rochester I would tell thee where thee could find a job. In four days I will tell thee."

Four days passed and Katie returned to the Willetses' house. The message she brought was: "Apply to William Wiley of the Auburn and Rochester Railroad, tomorrow at two o'clock, and thee will have a job before the week is out."

Willets asked Isaac Post to go with him to the railroad office. There William Wiley told them that there were no job openings. Nor did Wiley expect any to open in the near future. Willets and Post went back to Leah Fish's home and asked to see Katie.

Katie came in and sat down at a table across from the two men. She said nothing, but looked at them with large solemn eyes.

"I want to ask a question," Willets said. "It is: 'How is this? Mr. Wiley said he had no place for me.' "

Katie repeated the question in a low voice, as if talking to herself. Almost at once there were raps on the table between her and the two men. Very slowly the answer was worked out by counting the number of raps. The two men did the counting. Katie sat with a faraway look in her eyes. She did not seem to be paying any attention to what went on—nor did she seem to care.

The ghost's answer, as it worked out from the raps, was: "There will be a place for thee. Thee will know it before the week is out."

Willets at this point believed that the séances had all been guesswork by Katie or some helper who made the knocks. It was just an accident that they had been right about the land sale. Wiley had told him that there was no job open or any hope of one. Now the "ghost" was trying to tell him that he would have a job by Saturday night.

Isaac Post was a strong believer and argued with Willets. Willets agreed to see Wiley on Saturday, just in case something had changed. Again Wiley told him there was no job. Willets then followed up other leads for work. Finding none, he went home in the early evening. He was stunned when his wife told him that Wiley had come to the house. He wanted Willets to go to work immediately. A trusted employee had been caught in a dishonest act and had been fired. Although Willets was not the next name on the list, Wiley could not find any of the others on such short notice. He needed a man immediately. Willets took the job.

"Right then," he said later, "I became a believer in Spiritualism. And my belief has never wavered. I *know* Katie Fox really talked with my father after all."

Others had similar experiences and swore by the Fox sisters. However, there were many more who did not. A number of people came to the Fish house just to catch the girls in a fraud. They did not succeed, but did not become Spiritualists either. Some came as troublemakers. Often they would interrupt and cause disturbances before Katie or Margaretta could answer their questions.

Once, according to Emma Hardinge, the Spiritualist author, a group of rowdies became so threatening that the girls and their mother fled upstairs and locked their doors.

They had to threaten to send for the police before the angry men would leave the house.

Mrs. Fox and Margaretta wanted to quit after this. Leah broke into angry tears. She cried that this was the only way they could live. All of her piano pupils were gone, withdrawn by parents who believed that Spiritualism was a fake. She demanded that they go on giving paying séances. Katie Fox took her older sister's side. Margaretta, who did not have a strong character, was persuaded to change her mind when Katie argued with her. Mrs. Fox— very confused and fearful that they would be hurt—did not know what to do.

Leah argued that they had to return to Hydesville and dig up the body the ghost claimed was buried there.

"If the bones can be found," Leah argued, "then everyone will have to believe us."

"But what if no body is found in the cellar?" Mrs. Fox asked.

"Do you believe spirits are making those rappings? Do you think Katie and Margaretta are making them? Or me?"

"No, no," Mrs. Fox said. "I know something supernatural is making them. We searched the house. We did everything to find out where they came from."

"Then it is *spirits*!" Leah snapped. "And if it is spirits, then there has to be a body in the cellar of that Hydesville house. I intend to find it!"

°4°

The Bitter Tests

Leah, Mrs. Fox, and the two younger girls returned to Hydesville in late July. The water in the ground had sunk to the point where digging could be resumed in the cellar. However, David Fox wanted nothing more to do with the ghost. Leah Fox Fish became hysterical. She cried and again claimed that giving séances was her only means of making a living. She could not go back to teaching piano, for she could not get students.

David finally agreed. He got his brother-in-law Steve Smith and two other men to help. For some odd reason, John Fox did not help. Nor did he work with Spiritualism the rest of his life. He took some of the money his daughters made and bought a farm. There he lived quietly.

An angry mob of people gathered about the house as the four men worked. Katie and Margaretta held candles to provide light for the men to work in the dark cellar. Leah, Mrs. Fox, and Mrs. Redfield stood outside to keep angry people from intruding on the diggers. A furious man wildly accused them of insulting God by "fooling with the dead." Another yelled that they should drag the women out of the way and get the men. The digging ended on the first day without finding the body.

The diggers returned the next day. Leah, in her book, said the "spectators were becoming more and more excited. They crowded into the cellar. Some called us crazy. They reached over the heads of the women and spat upon and dropped sticks and stones on those who were digging."

The crowd suddenly went silent when the diggers produced some reddish hair, charcoal, lime, and a board. Sir Arthur Conan Doyle, in his *History of Spiritualism*, said they found a human bone. This was not true, for no bones were found until many years later.

The crowd remained quiet until after the diggers left. The small discovery disturbed them. They were fearful that the ghost's story might have been true after all. But later word was whispered around that it had been a trick. One story claimed that calf bones had been hidden in the hole by the diggers. They hoped to pass them off as human bones. This story, too, was false.

These untrue stories inflamed the crowd. They marched angrily out to David Fox's home. The rest of the family was in terror as the shouting mob approached the house. But David Fox faced them calmly.

"I don't know what you are seeking," he said to them. "But you are welcome to search the house, if you will do it quietly."

David's quiet manner and his good reputation in the community made the men ashamed. They quieted down and soon left.

The next day Leah and Katie returned to Rochester.

Mrs. Fox and Margaretta followed them a few days later. Leah insisted that the things they did find proved that there had been a real ghost in the Hydesville house. However, she was disappointed that they had not found a full skeleton and the tin peddler's box supposedly buried with the dead man.

None of the Fox family lived to see it, but a skeleton was eventually found in the Hydesville house cellar. Conan Doyle, in his book written in 1926, quoted a newspaper clipping that tells about it. The clipping was from the November 22, 1904, issue of the Boston *Journal*. It read:

> The skeleton of the man supposed to have caused the rappings first heard by the Fox sisters in 1848 has been found in the walls of the house occupied by the sisters, and clears them of the only shadow of doubt held concerning their sincerity in the discovery of spirit communication.
>
> The Fox sisters declared they learned to communicate with the spirit of a man, and that he told them he had been murdered and buried in the cellar. Repeated excavations failed to locate the body and thus give proof positive of their story.
>
> The discovery was made by schoolchildren playing in the "Spook House," where the Fox sisters heard the wonderful rappings. William H. Hyde, who owns the house, made an investigation and found an almost entire human skeleton between the earth and the crumbling cellar walls. It was undoubtedly that of the wandering peddler who it was claimed was murdered and whose body was hidden in the cellar. . . .

The Fox sisters did not know this when they returned to Rochester. But Leah was as determined as ever. She immediately began giving séances again. She charged a dollar a person for a sitting with Katie and Margaretta. Later she became a medium herself, but at this time she acted as manager for her younger sisters.

Soon after their return, E. W. Capron, the young Auburn businessman, asked Mrs. Fox to permit him to take Katie back to Auburn. Katie was eager to go. Her mother and Leah discussed it. Leah was opposed at first, but changed her mind. She wanted to broaden interest in Spiritualism and this seemed a good way to do it. Margaretta would continue to give séances in Rochester. Katie, under the sponsorship of Capron, could open up a new field in Auburn. Except for his closest friends, Capron agreed to charge those who came to see Katie. He would take no part of the money himself. It would all be sent back to Mrs. Fox in Rochester.

Katie was a big hit in Auburn. She was a very solemn young lady while at the séance table. But away from it she was lively and playful. Everyone liked her. Years later an old man told how he had attended a Katie Fox séance when he was fourteen. He described Katie as being quite pretty. A Currier and Ives print made about this time shows that he was right. He said that he winked at Katie and that she winked back at him.

But while Katie Fox was making a big hit in Auburn, trouble was building up for the Fox family in Rochester.

For some time the spirits had been urging the sisters to spread the word about Spiritualism. The spirits called for a large public meeting. Leah did not want to have one. Too many people were against Spiritualism. After a terrifying experience when a mob invaded their parlor, Leah had been careful not to let any strangers in to a séance. New visitors had to be introduced by a person known to Leah.

Leah discussed the idea of public lectures with her mother and Calvin Brown. Brown was a young man Leah and Mrs. Fox had asked to move into their house as protection for them after the mob forced the women to lock themselves in an upstairs room. Brown had known the Fox family for a number of years. For years he had begged Leah to marry him. Brown, who worked in a Rochester candy store, did not believe in ghosts at all. But because of his regard for Leah, he helped the best he could. The spirits, because he did not believe in them, disliked him. He was the constant butt of their jokes. They threw things at him, rumpled his hair, pulled his ears, and—while he was never hurt—annoyed him in many ways.

E. W. Capron and Isaac and Amy Post argued strongly for a public exhibition.

"It will make hundreds of new believers," Post argued. "If people could see and hear the raps, they would have to believe."

"So many people are against us," Leah replied.

"And every one of them is a person who has never attended a full séance," Capron replied. "They either have never seen Katie or Margaretta or have come here and caused trouble without sitting through the whole séance."

"Not a single person has ever sat through a full séance and left without a feeling of mystery," Post added. "I'll admit that many of them did not become Spiritualists, but everyone admitted that he or she *did not know how the raps were made*. This in itself gets them to thinking and in time they will join us too."

"I'll do it!" Leah said. "Where can we hold the exhibition?"

"I'll arrange to rent Corinthian Hall," Capron said. "That is the largest place in Rochester. I think we should put the admission charge at twenty-five cents. That will cover expenses and probably show a profit as well. We want to keep the price as low as possible, for the object is to get as many people in to hear the raps for themselves and to hear answers to questions that only a supernatural being can give."

It was decided then to hold the public meeting in the large hall as soon as there was an empty date. The public séance was finally set for the evening of November 14, 1849. The time was "7-and-a-half o'clock" and the price was twenty-five cents for one person or fifty cents for a "gentleman accompanied by two ladies."

Leah decided not to call Katie back from Auburn where she was doing so well. But E. W. Capron, Katie's sponsor there, hurried back to make the opening speech describing how Spiritualism works.

The advertising promised a "full explanation of the nature and history of the MYSTERIOUS NOISES supposed to be supernatural, which have caused so much excitement in this city . . . for the past two years. [Actually, it had been one year and eight months since the raps were first heard in the Hydesville house.] . . . The 'mysterious agencies' have promised to give the public an actual demonstration of the sounds, so that they may know that the sounds are neither made nor controlled by human beings."

The announcement caused wide discussion in Rochester. Most of it was angry. Threats were made against the Foxes and all those who "had truck with the witches!" Isaac Post became nervous about the harsh words he heard. He visited the chief of police and asked that policemen be sent to the hall just in case anyone tried to harm Leah and Margaretta. He did not tell the Foxes that he had taken this precaution. He did not want to add to their uneasiness. He also recruited several husky men to stand close to the stage in case there was trouble before the police could get there.

Capron was positive there would be no trouble. He told Post that once anyone sat through a full séance he or she could not fail to be impressed.

Post said he hoped that Capron was right, but he went on making his arrangements for trouble.

The month before this a man named C. Chauncey Burr had given a lecture in Corinthian Hall. He called his subject Electro-Biology. It was actually a demonstration of hypnotism. At this time Burr heard about the "Rochester Rappings." He asked to attend one of Margaretta's séances. Leah was suspicious of him and refused. Burr was enraged. Now he returned to Rochester to attend the public exhibition of the rapping. However, he was not interested in Spiritualism. He was seeking information he could use to attack the girls as fakes. In time Burr would become one of the bitterest enemies the girls ever had.

Leah and Margaretta's Spiritualist friends turned out to help the evening of the fourteenth. George Willets was the doorman. Others acted as ushers. Mrs. Amy Post and two other ladies took their places on the platform with Leah and Margaretta to give them moral support. E. W. Capron was selected to make the introduction.

Leah was thankful for their help, but angered because several other friends refused to appear in public with the Spiritualists. Also, the audience was smaller than she had expected. Only about 250 people bought tickets.

E. W. Capron opened the event. "I will give a simple and plain explanation of the 'spiritual telegraph,' " he said. "I will tell you how it began and how it grew to what it is tonight. I will not try to tell you what it is, but I will tell you what it is *not*. After I have finished speaking and you have heard a demonstration of the raps, then I will ask *you*, the audience, with no help from any of us who assist these earnest young ladies here tonight, to pick your own committee to investigate these mysterious noises.

"I assure you that Miss Fox—Margaretta—and her older sister, Mrs. Ann Leah Fish, will give full cooperation to your committee. Then I ask that *your* committee—men chosen by you from among you—report back here tomorrow night at this time. Then let us hear from them if they feel these ladies are sincere or not."

The audience had come to jeer, but Capron spoke so well that they remained quiet while he spoke. He told them about the house at Hydesville and its weird night noises. He went on to recount the story of Katie Fox challenging the knocker to repeat her own raps.

As he continued the story, raps began to sound in the auditorium. They were loud enough to be heard clearly by all in the hall. At important points in the story the knocks became very loud as if the unseen author of the raps was agreeing with the speaker.

At the end of his story, Capron asked questions which

were answered by raps. The raps did not appear to come from anywhere near Margaretta. The young girl sat quietly through Capron's speech. She did not appear to move at all. Her hands remained clasped in her lap. She was dressed in a black silk dress cut down from an old garment of Leah's. Her braided hair had been wound in buns over her ears in a grownup style, but this did not keep her from looking very young. She was then about thirteen or fourteen years old, but looked much younger sitting quietly beside her older sister.

The raps seemed to come from all over the stage. In a small room in a house, the raps seemed more mysterious and remarkable than they did in the large auditorium.

At the end of Capron's speech there were more spirit rappings and then the audience chose by vote the five men who would investigate the rapping. Those chosen were A. J. Combs, Daniel Marsh, A. Judson, Edwin Jones, and Nathaniel Clark.

It was then too late to work with the committee. Margaretta and Leah went home after agreeing to meet the committee the next morning. The girls were not to know the place until taken there by Nathaniel Clark. This was done so that they could not secretly bring in any machinery to help them make the raps, Clark explained. Leah agreed to the secrecy.

A reporter from the Rochester *Democrat* newspaper was so sure that the committee would find the girls a fake that he wrote about the "explosion of the rapping humbug." The editor set it aside to run in the paper after the committee made its report.

The editor and the four hundred people who came to the second meeting held the following night (November 15) were dumfounded when Nathaniel Clark gave the committee's report.

He told how the committee had selected the Sons of Temperance hall for the examination. "Sounds were heard on the floor near the two ladies," Clark said. "The sounds were very distinct. Then part of the committee heard rappings on the wall behind them. Then a number of questions were asked. These were answered by raps. The answers were not altogether right nor altogether wrong."

The committee was still not satisfied. They could see no way that either Leah or Margaretta could have made the raps. But just to make sure that one of their friends had not slipped into the building, the committee went to a private home.

"The sounds were heard on the outside of the front door while *we were all on the inside*," Clark went on. "Then they were heard on a closet door. When we put our hands on the door we could feel the jar of the raps. But when we opened the door there was no one on the other side.

"One of the committee put his hands upon the feet of the ladies. Another put his hands on the floor. Their feet were not moved, but there was a distinct jar of the floor when the raps sounded. We also heard the sounds upon the pavement outside and upon the ground as we left the house.

"Both ladies gave us full cooperation. They also said they would submit to a search by a committee of women if we thought they had some mechanical rapping machine hidden in their clothing.

"All members of the committee agreed that the sounds were heard, but *we entirely failed to discover any means by which the sounds could have been made.*"

When Clark stopped speaking the audience sat in surprised silence. Then sharp rapping noises sounded from the stage. It was as if the spirits were applauding the committee's report.

Then there was an explosion of angry voices. Some of the men in the audience jumped to their feet, shouting and shaking their fists in the air. Margaretta shrank back against her sister. Leah put her arms protectingly about the younger girl. Capron, Post, and Willets moved closer to the women, so they could protect them if necessary.

Clark angrily called for order. A man in the audience yelled out that the entire committee had been bewitched by "these godless women." Another yelled that Margaretta was no better than the witch of Endore. This was the woman in the Bible whom King Saul forced to use magic to call up the spirit of the prophet Samuel. Clark tried to defend himself and the committee. Another angry voice demanded that a new committee be appointed. The audience roared in approval. Clark asked for nominations for the new committee.

Five well-known men were finally selected. The two most important were Dr. H. H. Langworthy, a medical instructor, and Frederick Whittlesey, a local educator.

Whittlesey, ignoring Leah, asked Margaretta if she would submit to another examination. The girl looked helplessly at her sister. Leah set her mouth in a straight hard line.

"We have nothing to hide," Leah said, her eyes flashing. "Just tell us where to be."

"Please—" Margaretta whispered in a stricken voice.

"We *must!*" Leah replied in a low tone that Whittlesey could hear, but which the audience could not. "If we refuse, our enemies will say we have something to hide."

Margaretta bowed her head to hide the tears glistening in her eyes. "I wish Katie was with me," she whispered.

The examination of Clark's committee had been much harder for her than anyone realized. The exact details of it were not put down, but Emma Hardinge, who knew the Fox sisters, wrote, "Their feelings were outraged. Their statements doubted. Their sensitive natures were wounded to agony by the cold, severe, and often sneering scrutiny to which they were subjected." Mrs. Hardinge added that the girls could not have endured the examination except for the support of their living friends and the encouragement of the spirits themselves.

The investigation by the new committee was even harder on Leah and Margaretta than the first had been. It was held in the offices of Chancellor Whittlesey to ensure that no confederate helped make the raps. In addition to the chosen committee members, Whittlesey brought a friend who was visiting him. This man was Supreme Court Justice John W. Edmonds.

Later Justice Edmonds became one of the most important names in early Spiritualism. But at this meeting he—like the others—believed that the rappings were a fraud. In a book he wrote in 1854, the justice described the examination of Margaretta:

Justice John W. Edmonds.

As I entered the room, she [Margaretta] was seated at one side of the table. The rappings came with a hurried, cheerful sound on the floor where I sat. I had taken my seat on the opposite side of the table. I listened with the idea in my mind that she was doing it with her feet, or hands, or knee joints.

Directly the sounds were heard on the table, and not on the floor. They were in a place her hands could not reach. It was ventriloquism, I said to myself. I put my hands on the table directly over the sounds. I distinctly felt the vibration as if a hammer had been struck. It was machinery, I imagined. Then the sounds moved around the table. The vibration followed my hands wherever I put them.

The committee interrupted the séance at this point to turn the table over and inspect it for hidden machinery that might have been used to make the raps. They found nothing.

Dr. Langworthy also thought that either Leah or Margaretta was using ventriloquism to make the noise. Even then ventriloquism or "voice throwing" was a very old showman's trick. The ventriloquist talks deep in his throat without moving his lips. Then by directing the audience's attention to a different place——often the moving lips of a dummy——it appears to his listeners as if the noise came from there. Langworthy put his stethoscope against the chest first of Leah and then of Margaretta while the rapping was going on.

After listening to their breathing, the doctor told the others, "It is certainly not ventriloquism. Their breathing is normal."

In the end the new committee reported to the assembly the next day that it had investigated the rapping thoroughly. "We can say positively that they were not made by ventriloquism or any machinery. We are not able to say what the agency was that made the sounds."

The antispiritualists exploded with rage. A man named Lewis Burtis jumped to his feet shouting, "I would expose this fraud in minutes if I were on the committee. But those girls would never permit *me* to examine them!"

Another man named Lafe Kenyon shouted that if he were put on the committee he would discover the secret of the raps or would throw himself over Genesee Falls (the waterfalls in the river that cuts through Rochester).

The angry crowd demanded still another investigation

and elected Burtis and Kenyon as members. Dr. Langworthy was asked to serve again, and two other new members were added.

Although every member of the committee was violently opposed to Spiritualism, the men promised to make an honest examination. They also asked that a committee of women be appointed to search the girls' clothing.

At the twentieth anniversary observation of the Hydesville rappings held in 1868, Mrs. Amy Post told the gathering what happened that day in 1849 during the fourth examination of Margaretta Fox and her sister Leah.

There was a long discussion among the Spiritualists as to whether they should go back this fourth time. They finally agreed that it was necessary. The examination, headed by Burtis and Kenyon, was very difficult for Margaretta. After both Burtis and Kenyon announced that the rappings baffled them, a committee of three women took Margaretta and Leah into an adjoining room. Their friends were not permitted to go with them. They were forced to take off all their clothes, including their stockings and underwear. Leah submitted with dignity. Margaretta, who was so modest that she would not undress even before her sisters, was mortified with embarrassment.

The women searched the spiritualists' clothing and even stuck pins in the seams to make sure they had nothing hidden inside that could be used to make the mysterious raps. Finding nothing, they turned to Margaretta and Leah, examining their bodies. Margaretta, according to Emma Hardinge, "wept bitterly during this ordeal. But her sobs and cries were heard by her friends who had been excluded from the room. One of these—a sweet Quaker lady, Amy

Post—forced her way into the room where the poor girls were disrobed for the examination."

Weeping loudly, Margaretta threw herself into Mrs. Post's arms. Her friend, shaking with rage, accused the committee women of obscene actions. She grabbed up Margaretta's underclothes and pressed them into the sobbing girl's hands.

"Get dressed!" she said. "I'm taking you and Leah home. We'll have no more of this terrible treatment."

The committee women did not object. Nor did the men, including Burtis and Kenyon, who had been so sure that they could expose the secret of the rappings.

These examinations were made in the afternoon. Leah and Margaretta were supposed to return to Corinthian Hall in the evening when the reports of the committees would be read to the audience. Margaretta wept at the thought of going back, but Leah insisted that it was necessary.

Then word got around that these two committees, like the previous ones, had failed to find the secret of the rappings. Violent anti-Spiritualists started to make threats. One loudly claimed that they should lynch both Margaretta and Leah because "they are witches in league with the devil himself!"

The Fury of the Mob

The Spiritualists had a long argument about whether they should risk going back to Corinthian Hall that evening. Leah was firmly in favor of going.

"It would be cowardice not to go," she argued. "These ruffians will take it as proof that we have something to hide."

E. W. Capron, who knew of Isaac Post's precautions, also thought they should go back this last time. Margaretta, however, wept and said she would never go back to that "awful place."

A. H. Jervis, a Methodist minister who had joined the Spiritualist group, said, "I am not afraid to face a frowning world."

"If you will go, I will go with you," Leah said.

Isaac Post and George Willets also said they would go. Amy Post said she would not let Leah go without her. In thus agreeing to go back to Corinthian Hall, the entire group showed remarkable courage. Mob leaders were now threatening to lynch "not only the Fox witches, but all those who support them!"

The group agreed that Margaretta should not go, feeling as she did about it. Leah was not then a medium and could not draw raps from the spirits. However, Capron did not think this important.

"Three committees have now heard the raps and so have the audiences," he said. "They don't need to hear them again. With Leah there, the Fox family is represented. That is all we need."

Katie, of course, was still in Auburn. But none of the records of the Corinthian Hall meetings mention the mother, Margaret Fox. She was not at the hall during any of the examinations or audiences.

As evening approached and the determined little group of Spiritualists made ready to go to the hall, Margaretta had a change of mind. "I can't let you go without me," she said. Then she added in a low voice, "But I expect to be killed!"

Amy Post, in her speech to the twentieth anniversary meeting in 1868, reported this fear of Margaretta's. She said that the girl's agreeing to go in spite of this fear was the bravest act she had ever seen.

Mrs. Post, her husband Isaac, Leah, and the Reverend Jervis accompanied Margaretta to the stage and sat with her. George Willets had reduced the admission price to twenty cents from the original quarter of a dollar. This was done in order to get more people to attend. He hoped to attract more poorer people. He thought they favored Spiritualism more.

Margaretta looked very small and young, sitting pale-faced between the grim adults on each side of her. She was then somewhere between twelve and fourteen, depending upon whose story of her age one wishes to believe.

E. W. Capron tried to open the meeting as he had done before. He was shouted down by angry voices in the crowd. They demanded that the godless believer in spirits be removed. A Major Packard got up in the audience and moved that the audience pick its own chairman. Cheers followed his demand. The rowdy audience then voted to make J. W. Brissell, a local merchant, chairman of the meeting.

Packard escorted Brissell to the stage. Packard was red-faced, overweight, and had gray hair. Instead of going back to his seat, he stayed to make a short speech.

"You know that I was chosen to be a member of the investigating committee," he shouted, waving his arms as he spoke. "But the so-called spirits said they would not speak if I was present. I graciously bowed out, but I suspected these godless people did not want me because they knew I could not be fooled!

"I tell you that 'talking with the dead' is either a fake or blasphemy! In the Bible we read of a woman who called up the dead. This was when King Saul, afraid he was going to be defeated by his enemies, forced the woman of Endore to call up the ghost of Samuel to read the future.

"I tell you that the Bible called this woman of Endore a witch! And also heaven wreaked its vengeance upon the wicked Saul for daring to disturb the dead! Saul was killed along with his sons and his kingdom passed to King David, of blessed memory.

"I ask you, in light of what the Bible tells us about the wickedness of those who would disturb the honorable dead, should we allow such things to happen here in our own fair city?

"Let us hear what our committee has to say. But if they fail us, as the others have done, then I say, it is time for us to take matters into our own hands!"

Major Packard, walking as stiffly as a soldier on parade, marched back to his seat. The audience cheered loudly. His stern face relaxed into a pleased smile as he took his seat. It was plain to all that the major was very satisfied with himself.

Margaretta sat very quietly during Packard's tirade. She seemed to be in a trance. Leah's lips were pressed tightly together. It was as if she was trying to keep from shouting back at Packard.

Brissell then talked with the committee. He was told that they did not have a group report, but that each member would tell what he had seen.

The first to speak was Lewis Burtis. He was a man in his twenties. He had claimed that the Fox sisters were afraid to have him on the committee. He had loudly promised to expose the fraud.

Now he was subdued. His face was red with embarrassment. He shuffled his feet uneasily. Before beginning to speak he turned and looked at Margaretta. She did not look back at him.

Then in a quiet voice Burtis told the audience how the committee had met Leah and Margaretta at 9:30 AM in the Rochester House, a leading hotel. The investigation lasted most of the day.

Someone set off firecrackers in the audience. Chairman Brissell warned against any more disturbances. He also told some people in the front row to stop crackling peanut shells. It made noise that kept people in the rear from hearing the speaker.

Burtis went on to describe the investigation. He pointed out that three ladies had searched the mediums, but had found no secret rap-making machines on them.

The women on the committee refused to appear on stage. It would not be proper, they insisted. However, they had prepared a written report which Burtis read. The report described their search of the girls and ended with the words, "When the girls were standing on pillows, with a handkerchief tied around the bottom of their dresses, tight to the ankles, we all heard the rapping on the wall and the floor distinctly."

Burtis concluded by saying that he was absolutely unable to say how the rapping noises were made. He added that he was sure of one thing: They were not made by Margaretta Fox or her sister Leah.

There was a roar of angry voices. The crowd was not large. Only 280 people had showed up. (One newspaper claimed there were 1,500, but E. W. Capron, who was there, said this was wrong.)

The next to report was L. Kenyon, the man who had said he would throw himself over Genesee Falls if he failed to expose the fraud. He had to confess that he had not done so. He agreed with Burtis that neither Margaretta nor Leah could have made the raps without being detected.

Jeers answered the red-faced Kenyon. He was accused of having been bewitched by the "Rochester witches." William Fitzhugh then arose to make his report. The rowdy crowd would not let him speak. They kept shouting and setting off firecrackers. They yelled for Fitzhugh to get off the stage. The committee was a failure. The audience would take matters into its own hands.

Fitzhugh, a tough Irishman, yelled back that he would not sit down. He intended to have his say if it took all night. However, the noise continued until he angrily grabbed his hat and left.

Major Packard jumped upon a seat and yelled for attention. Cheers and a volley of exploding firecrackers greeted him.

"The false committee we elected may not know how the infernal rapping was done," he yelled. "But I do! These wicked women have lead balls sewed in the hems of their dresses. They make the noises by moving so the balls hit the floor!"

Capron tried to point out that Margaretta and Leah's dresses had been searched by the ladies' committee. No one would listen to him. They cheered Packard.

Margaretta got nervously to her feet. Mrs. Post stood up with her. The men were already on their feet. Leah remained seated. She was like a woman of iron. Her lips were set in a grim line. She stared straight ahead.

"I'll prove what I say!" Packard shouted. "Come on! We'll inspect their dresses ourselves!"

Packard started for the stage. A dozen rowdies fell in behind him. George Willets, his angry face mirroring his outrage, moved in front of Margaretta.

"If you touch her, it will be over my dead body!" he cried.

E. W. Capron also moved in front of Leah and Margaretta. Reverend Jervis, the other man on the stage with them, hurried off to get the police, who were waiting back of the stage.

The police moved in quickly, brandishing clubs. Packard and his rowdies paused. The rest of the audience jeered. A new round of firecrackers were set off. The police detail closed around Leah and Margaretta. They hurried the girls off the stage and out through the back door. The chief of the detail, S. W. Moore, sent one of his men hurrying back to the police station to alert more men in case they were needed.

Willets and Reverend Jervis accompanied the women. Moore advised against returning to Leah's home. He thought the mob might try to follow them there. They agreed to go to the Post home. Moore left a small police detail to guard the place. He also arranged for larger police details to be sent out if the angry mob tried to storm the Post home.

The angry crowd did not follow. They remained in Corinthian Hall while Major Packard and others inflamed them with speeches. Capron remained behind, staying on the outside of the group, to hear what was being said. In this way he could alert the police if there was a sign that the men intended to carry out their threat to "lynch the spirit witches."

However, the presence of the police and their guard around the women had dampened this idea. There was no more talk of lynching. But they voted a resolution ordering the Fox family to leave Rochester within twenty-four hours. Capron reported this to Leah later that night.

"We are not leaving!" she snapped.

However, she was afraid that trouble might spread to Auburn. Katie was staying in the boarding house where Capron lived when he was in that town. Leah told Capron that Katie should return to Rochester where they could all be together. Capron agreed. He said he would bring Katie back the next day.

In the meantime, the shouting crowd at the Corinthian Hall marched down Troup Street where Leah's house was located. They surrounded the place, yelling and shouting. At one point they threatened to burn it down. The police arrived and Moore threatened to arrest them all if they did not leave. After trading a few insults with Moore, the mob drifted away.

All threats against the Spiritualists' lives were just threats. Nothing more happened in Rochester, even though Leah immediately opened her home to new séances. The charge was a dollar a person and the house was always crowded.

However, there was a threat to Margaretta the following year. She had gone to Troy, New York. Katie carried on the séances in Rochester. Leah, who was learning to be a medium, helped in a small way. In Troy, Margaretta was staying with a Spiritualist believer who wrote a fearful letter to a friend in Rochester. He wrote:

> . . . We are trying to make an arrangement for Margaretta to go to another place to stay. Do not mention it to others, as you value her life. A deep plot is laid to destroy her. My house is beset every night by assassins after her. We guard her every moment.
>
> In returning from Troy, late the night before last, with my family and Margaretta, in a coach, we came to the river and found no boat. Five Irishmen tried to persuade our driver to go to the long "Troy bridge," a glorious place for murder.
>
> We did not go, but they followed us home. After we had retired, they tried to break into the room occupied by Margaretta and my sister-in-law.

They were furious on being foiled, and threw stones against the house. I have prepared means of defense, and cannot sleep much. I fear they will return again tonight. They will receive a warm reception.

Last night Mrs. B [his sister-in-law] and Margaretta went to the door of a shed together. A stone was thrown at them. The men are large and stout.

The writer did not immediately mail the letter and had time to add a postscript the next day:

As I feared, the Irishmen did return last night. They threw stones through the window and broke into the house.

Leah rushed to Troy as soon as this letter was received. She was met by fearful Spiritualists. They disguised her and took her to a hotel where they had her register under another name. She was told that it was too dangerous for another Fox sister to be in the town.

Emma Hardinge wrote: "The ladies [Leah and Margaretta] were finally taken in safety and secrecy to Albany. There a better reception awaited them. Then it was found that the Irish and Catholics did *not* make up the bulk of the rude and jibing mob that surrounded Mr. Bouton's house, fired shots and threw stones at the windows, uttering threats against the 'unholy witch woman within.'" The mob was made up of angry townspeople, with race and individual religious faith playing no part in their fury.

Margaretta had been frightened half to death. But the kindness she found in Albany revived her own spirits. She stopped pleading with Leah to stop the séances.

° 6 °

The Spread of Spiritualism

The harsh examinations and disorder in Corinthian Hall had been frightening. But they
turned out to be just the thing that Leah needed to arouse
interest in Spiritualism.

Local newspapers had carried stories about the Hydesville rappings, but these were treated like a joke. The
Corinthian Hall examinations, in which such prominent
citizens were unable to prove the Fox sisters fakes, aroused
tremendous interest. Papers all over the country carried
stories about the curious "Rochester Rappings."

Many papers continued to treat the rappings as a joke or
a hoax. Others decried them as work of the devil, as the
mobs in Rochester and Troy had done. One paper said,
"Committees of men of the highest standing cannot tell
whence the noise came, nor how it is made. And it is no
marvel that they cannot, for the Bible is not their guide.
Would they look into that neglected book, the mystery
would at once be solved. They would learn that this spirit,
which seems to be an associate of certain women, is of the
same character as the *familiar spirits* so frequently spoken
of and condemned in the Bible."

Many people were attracted to Spiritualism because they had lost beloved members of their family. It eased their pain to be told by Leah Fox Fish that "there is no death!" Judge Edmonds was one of these. After being present at the first examination of Margaretta, Edmonds came back several times and then became an ardent Spiritualist. The same thing happened to Lewis Burtis—the man who first claimed that Leah did not dare to have him on the committee that investigated Margaretta. Burtis became a strong believer in Spiritualism after that and told of his conversion at the twentieth anniversary meeting in 1868. Hundreds of others came to see the Fox sisters. The house was always full of people—at a dollar each.

After word of the "Rochester Rappings" got around, others claimed to have heard ghostly raps also. None had admitted this before, they said, either because they were afraid or because they did not realize where the sounds were coming from until Katie and Margaretta showed the way.

Spiritualists also pointed out that shortly before the Hydesville ghost appeared, Andrew Jackson Davis, the famed mystic, predicted in a book that the living would soon talk to the dead. Going farther back in history, they recalled that the noted European scientist and mystic Emanuel Swedenborg claimed the ability to talk with the dead.

Suddenly hundreds of other people claimed to be spirit mediums. Mediums became so common that eighteen months after the Corinthian Hall exhibitions the New Hampshire House of Representatives adopted a resolution. It said that "the committee on the Judiciary should inquire into the need of a law for protecting the people of the state from injury by persons pretending to hold intercourse with departed spirits."

Frank Podmore, in his history of early Spiritualism, said, "The new sect [of Spiritualism] grew rapidly. . . . Hammon speaks of 2,000 writing mediums alone in 1852 . . . whilst a few years later it was stated, on accurate and very reliable information, that the Spiritualists numbered eleven million."

Curiously, many of the new mediums were young people. One of these was the ten-year-old daughter of Anson Attwood, of Troy, New York. The young girl developed into a medium soon after Margaretta Fox's first visit to the town.

A group of investigators, headed by a General Bullard, called at the Attwood home to see the young medium. They found her playing with her dolls. She did not want to perform for the visitors and became quite cross when they insisted. Her mother explained that the child had been disturbed by so many people that she did not want to be bothered anymore.

One of the committee (whose name was not recorded) bribed the girl by offering her candy. This angered General Bullard. He said he had not come to play games with children. He suggested they call the investigation off. The others insisted on going ahead.

The Attwood girl, the group discovered, did not talk with ghosts like the Fox sisters did. Instead, the spirits acted through her. According to Emma Hardinge, "Seated on a high chair, the young medium all unconsciously munched her sweetmeats while the spirits lifted her about. They moved her from place to place with the ease of a feather blown by the wind.

"Meanwhile the heavy table around which the party had gathered rocked and rolled like a ship at sea. The chairs of the gentlemen, with their occupants, were moved bodily."

At the same time, raps about the room began spelling out messages from dead relatives and friends of the investigators. The little girl claimed to have nothing to do with the rappings.

Mrs. Hardinge reported that the investigators soon forgot the "youth and insignificance of the little *telegraphic wire* that the spirits were using." By this time mediums had become known as "spiritual telegraphs." Samuel F. B. Morse had invented the telegraph a few years before, and many thought that Spiritualism was based upon the same idea. The spiritual rapping was compared to the dot-dash clicks of the telegraph. Those advancing this theory claimed that mediums had bodily electricity which the spirits used in the same way that Morse's telegraph used electrical current to work its telegraph key.

The committee, awed by the supposed supernatural things that the ten-year-old medium caused, forgot that they were supposed to expose her as a trickster. Then close to the end of the séance, the ghostly presence of General Bullard's brother sent a message. The general made one last effort to check before he agreed that spirits were really at work. Mrs. Hardinge's account claims:

> The general *mentally* framed this sentence:
> "If this be indeed the spirit of my brother, let him move that child in her chair toward me."
> . . . The child, chair and all, were lifted, carried, or moved, none present could define how, completely round

the table and set lightly down by the side of General Bullard.

The group was speechless. Then General Bullard jumped to his feet, crying, "By Heaven, it is all true!"

The group had come to see the little girl at the insistence of their minister. This man was violently opposed to the idea of Spiritualism. He was angry when the group reported back to him that they believed the Attwood girl could work with spirits. He insisted that he could not be hoodwinked as they had been. He visited the Attwood home. He came away so impressed that he later became a medium himself.

The records do not show what happened to the Attwood girl after this. But records do show that many other children and young people acted as mediums.

N. P. Tallmadge, a U.S. senator and former governor of Wisconsin, claimed that his ten-year-old daughter had a spirit friend who helped her with her piano lessons. With the spirit's help, she played difficult classical pieces that she could not play alone.

A teenage girl in New York became almost as famous as the Fox sisters. Her name was Cora Hatch. She first became known under the name of Cora Scott when she was fifteen years old. She was perhaps the prettiest of all the mediums of her time. Her shoulder-length blond hair was curled in ringlets. She had large soulful blue eyes and a full red mouth. She was very quiet and modest in manner.

Miss Scott was a trance medium. While in a trance she gave speeches that many thought more profound than any preacher's. Later she married her manager, John Hatch, and became known as Cora Hatch.

Some whispered that Miss Scott was not as young as people thought. When she was seventeen a reporter for a New York newspaper said she had probably not been seventeen for *more* than three years.

Anyway, Miss Scott was very pretty and people flocked to see her. She did not do rappings or make chairs move about. She just talked, claiming that while in her trance the spirits spoke through her voice.

Two other famous teenage mediums were the Davenport brothers. Like the Fox sisters, it is hard to tell how old Ira and William Davenport were. Harry Houdini, the famous magician, said that Ira was ten and William was eight when they first heard of the Corinthian Hall meeting. Others have claimed that they were teenagers.

In any event, the two boys and their younger sister, Elizabeth, were disturbed by rapping noises two years before the ghost of the murdered man rapped his messages to the Fox sisters in Hydesville. No attention was paid to this until after the Corinthian Hall meeting spread the fame of Spiritualism.

The children lived in Buffalo, New York. Their father was a policeman. Soon after they heard about the Fox sisters, strange things began to happen in the Davenport house. Conan Doyle says that once the silverware on the table began to dance. The table was lifted into the air, and strange noises were heard.

In their teens Ira and William developed a stage act. They built a spirit cabinet. In company with a man named Fay, the brothers were securely tied by members of the audience. They were then placed in the cabinet along with a member of the audience who sat between them. The cabinet door was then closed. Immediately musical instruments inside the cabinet were played. Unseen hands pulled at the observer from the audience who was inside with the tied-up brothers. Then when Fay opened the cabinet doors, the brothers were found still tied up.

The observer swore that they had not moved. Members of the audience were called up to inspect the knots in the ropes, which had been sealed with wax. They were intact.

The Davenport brothers became quite famous. They later went to England, France, and Germany, where they displayed their spirit cabinet.

The most famous of all the young mediums inspired by the Fox sisters was Daniel Dunglas Home. Home was seventeen years old when Margaretta and Leah Fox got so much publicity from the Corinthian Hall meeting. Home claimed that he did not hear about this, although he admitted that his aunt knew about the "Rochester rappers."

Home was born in Scotland in 1833, but came to the United States with his aunt when he was nine years old. He had several mystic experiences in his childhood. When he was thirteen the ghost of a young friend appeared to him. Earlier the two boys had made a pledge that whichever of them died first would show himself as a ghost to the other.

Then in 1850, six months after the November Corinthian Hall meeting in 1849, Daniel awoke his aunt in the night. He told her that the ghost of his mother (with whom he had not lived since he was nine) had appeared to him. His mother's spirit told the boy that she had died at twelve o'clock that day while visiting friends.

His aunt refused to believe him, but the next day she received a message that her sister had died exactly as Daniel had said. Shortly after this, their home was disturbed by loud rappings and knocks like those reported by the Fox sisters.

Daniel's aunt was greatly disturbed. There were three different churches in town. She got a minister from each one to save her nephew from the ghosts. When this did not work, she accused him of bringing the devil into her house. She told him to leave. He did—starting out at seventeen as a spiritualist medium.

Unlike the Fox sisters, Home refused to take any money for his séances. He lived as a house guest with different people, moving on as he chose. Later he went to England, France, and Italy, becoming the most famous Spiritualist of his time.

He did more than just act as the medium through which spirits could talk with the living. He gave amazing exhibitions of what many thought were occult powers. It was claimed that he could stretch his body, gaining as much as a full foot of extra height. He could float in the air, rising up to touch the ceiling of a room. Sir William Crookes, the famous British scientist, told of seeing Home stoop down before a fireplace and put his face in the fire. Yet the medium was not burned. Home then picked up a live coal in his hands and was still not burned. Lord Adare, a British nobleman, told of seeing Home float out a third-story window of a house and then float back in again through another window in a different room.

These things sound impossible. Yet famous people swore they saw them. Elizabeth Barrett Browning, the poetess, believed ardently in Home. Her husband, the famous poet Robert Browning, hated Home and tried to destroy his reputation. Harry Houdini, the famous American magician, claimed everything Home did was a trick. He claimed he could duplicate every trick. However, when asked to do Home's trick of floating out a three-story-high window and back in another one, Houdini failed to do so. A date was set for him to try—under the same conditions as Home had done—but Houdini called the demonstration off. He said his assistant was sick.

Children and young people who attracted the spirits did not always have a good time of it. A Presbyterian minister named Phelps married a widow with four children: two girls, aged sixteen and six, and two boys, aged eleven and three. The children developed the spiritual magnetism that attracts spirits, or so it was claimed. Unfortunately, the spirits they attracted were far different from the kindly ones who worked through the Fox sisters and others. They were wicked and malicious.

It was claimed that the oldest boy was hung in a tree and his pantaloons stripped from him. A piece of tape was tightly wound around the oldest girl's neck as she slept. She was almost strangled. A potato dropped out of the air at the breakfast table, almost hitting Dr. Phelps. The three-year-old boy was picked up and carried across the room. A newspaperman came and heard loud raps that shook the house.

Many other strange things happened. Phelps—believing that the children's magnetism drew the spirits—sent the older boy off to boarding school. The spirits followed. They destroyed his books, tore his clothing, and made such a noisy disturbance that the school sent him back home.

Dr. Phelps asked the famous Andrew Jackson Davis to

witness these strange things and to sign a certificate that they really happened. Phelps also consulted Leah Fox. Leah said the damage was being done by insane spirits. E. W. Capron said that he had been told by a spirit that one could not always believe what every spirit said. Death, this spirit told Capron, did not change one's personality. If a person was stupid, mean, or spiteful in life, he or she would be the same as a spirit. This, Capron said, accounted for the malicious treatment of the Phelps children.

As hundreds of new mediums appeared and hundreds of thousands of people flocked to see them, it was natural that many crooks and frauds appeared. One woman arranged a loose board under her chair. Then with her foot she could create knocks. Another was exposed when investigators found that she had worked a small lead ball into the heel of her shoe.

Another woman had a clever trick. She would permit only believers in Spiritualism to her séances. Then through clever talk she would get them excited. At this point she would scream: "They are here! They are all around us. They are gradually taking form! Can't you see them glowing like mist in the dark! Can't you *see* them!"

And so great was her excitement that she actually convinced her sitters that they saw something that was not there at all.

As Spiritualism got moving, new mediums brought in new ideas. Just plain rapping was no longer a novelty. The first to improve on Katie and Margaretta's rappings was their friend E. W. Capron. It was very slow work reciting the entire alphabet while the spirit rapped yes or no for each letter. Capron wrote the alphabet on a large card and pointed to each letter. This speeded up the messages and was the origin of the Ouija board. This board has the letters of the alphabet printed on it, along with the words *yes* and *no*. A small marker is moved to each letter—presumably by the spirit—to spell out the message.

Some mediums started using phosphorescent material that glowed in the dark to create ghostly images. Spirit music was invented. The first known case of a ghost playing a tune at a séance was in Auburn, New York. Katie Fox had introduced Spiritualism there while the guest of E. W. Capron. As soon as Katie blazed the way, a number of women in the town claimed to be mediums also. One of these had ghostly harp and piano music playing in the background while the rappings went on.

After this, music became an important part of séances. Guitars floated around the room, apparently unheld by any human hands, and played themselves. The famous D. D. Home showed a self-playing accordion during his European séances. A report from California tells how Andronico Vallejo, son of the famous grandee General Vallejo, became very angry when a spirit floated his prize guitar out of the house.

With so many fake mediums being exposed, it was natural that enemies of Spiritualism should try every means of exposing the Fox sisters, for they were the ones who started it all.

None of these would-be exposers was successful. However, they repeated many stories (all of them false) to account for the Fox rappings. One story printed in an Auburn newspaper claimed that the original rappings in the Hydesville house had been made by John Fox. This story said Fox made the sounds by sitting a certain way on a creaky bedstead.

Capron asked sarcastically, "Does the writer wish us to believe that Mr. Fox carried the bedstead down into the cellar so we could hear the sound there?"

Actually, John Fox—after his first experience in the Hydesville house—had nothing more to do with Spiritualism.

Since John and Margaret Fox and the Reverend Jervis were all staunch members of the Methodist church, other members of the religion were constantly asked about the church's position on Spiritualism. A church paper made a clear statement:

> No one can deny the possibility of our being visited by inhabitants of the invisible state. The possibility of such a thing, however, does not authorize us to lay aside our senses. . . .
>
> Both good and evil spirits have access to this lower world. They doubtless have much to do with the actions of men. But their influence is ordinarily disguised. These spirits act upon our being through the agency of another, as Satan did through the serpent when he tempted Eve. . . .
>
> We have thus far believed the rappings to be sheer imposture, not worth going a rod to see, nor deserving the slightest notice from the press. . . . The devil is not a fool. If he is really the author—a fact we are not disposed to question—of these strange communications, we imagine there is some intervening agency to share with him the guilt of such silly falsehood.

What the author of this editorial seems to have been trying to say in a lot of unnecessary words is: "Katie and

Margaretta Fox, along with all other mediums, are fakes inspired by the devil."

Many agreed with the editorial writer, of course. But many people of high position and intelligence were interested in making a fair and honest test of the Spiritualists' claims.

One of these was Horace Greeley, the famous editor of the New York *Tribune*. Soon after the Corinthian Hall publicity spread the fame of Margaretta Fox, Greeley sent one of his reporters to Rochester to observe the "Rochester Rappings." The famous editor listened thoughtfully to the reporter's account.

Greeley's young son had died shortly before this. The editor and his wife Mary had talked about Spiritualism. She wondered if she could really talk with her dead child's spirit. Greeley did not really believe in it himself. But he had an open mind. He promised his wife he would investigate.

He questioned the reporter, George Ripley, who said that he had watched closely, for he suspected trickery.

"But I swear that the raps came from all over the room," he told Greeley. "I cannot see any possible way that those young girls could have made them."

"Could the raps have been made by someone working with them?" Greeley asked.

Ripley shook his head. "A lot of people have thought that," he said. "I'm told that it has been checked out. At the end of the séance I stood by the door. The raps sounded *on the door*. No one rapped on it on my side. I jerked the door open. There was no one on the other side either. *You* tell me who made the raps."

Greeley was silent for a moment, thinking. Then he said, "Do you really think these children talk to ghosts?"

Ripley shook his head. "All I can truthfully say, Mr. Greeley, is that I could not *prove* that they did not. And I tried."

"I would like very much to talk with these spirit rappers myself," Greeley said thoughtfully. "I think I shall invite them to come to New York."

But someone else—a man much more famous than Greeley—had the same idea. This man was the greatest "humbugger" who ever lived. His name was P. T. Barnum.

7

The Fox Trappers

Phineas Taylor Barnum was a showman, the father of modern extravagant press agentry. Even in his own day he was called the king of humbugs. Humbug, a popular slang term then, meant fake or something false. The word, unlike so much slang, survives to this day because of Scrooge's "Bah! Humbug!" reference to Christmas in Dickens' *A Christmas Carol.* But Barnum was more than just a faker. He was one of the most remarkable showmen America ever had.

Barnum was born in 1810. He began his business life as a store clerk. He worked hard and saved his money to open a small place of his own. Then in 1835 he was offered an aged black woman slave. She was supposed to be 136 years old and the childhood nurse of George Washington. For all her age, the woman could still tell a good story. She told how she had nursed baby George and what kind of a child he was. In fact, she told the story so well that Barnum quickly made back the $1,000 he paid for the right to exhibit her in a traveling show. He went on to make a considerable profit before she died in 1836, after eighteen months with Barnum.

The budding showman took this profit and bought an interest in a small circus. He was given the position of secretary-treasurer. He was paid $30 a week and one-fifth of the profits.

The show prospered, due to Barnum's flair for publicity. He made enough to buy Scudder's American Museum in 1841. This was a large building at the corner of Broadway and Ann Street in New York City. It exhibited various kinds of freaks and animals. Business was only fair until Barnum met a twenty-five-inch-high midget named Charles Stratton. Barnum hired Stratton and renamed him General Tom Thumb. He was an instant hit.

Barnum's Museum became one of the most famous showplaces in the world. He was constantly finding new and unusual attractions. Once he had a huge tank on wheels made and exhibited a real whale in it. He was the first to show Siamese twins—two Siamese boys whose bodies were joined together. Jumbo, the world's largest elephant, was one of his attractions.

All of these, of course, were real. But among them he also exhibited some of the most outrageous fakes of the time. This did not bother Barnum. He said that people liked to be humbugged. He added some words that have become famous: "There is one born every minute." He meant a sucker. Later he formed the famous Barnum and Bailey Circus. It joined with Ringling Brothers to become the Greatest Show on Earth.

A man like Barnum would naturally prick up his ears at something like talking with ghosts. He sent a secret representative to Rochester to report to him about the "Rochester Rappers" that the newspapers were talking about. He then had a representative approach Margaret Fox about her three daughters' appearing at the Barnum's American Museum. Mrs. Fox did not think it dignified for her daughters to appear in such a place.

Instead, Leah and Calvin Brown, the young man Leah later married, arranged for Margaretta and Katie to tour various towns in upstate New York. The two girls, with Leah accompanying them, made as much as a hundred dollars a day. Their expenses were high. They stayed at the best hotels and often had to hire bodyguards to protect them. Even so, the profit was enormous for the times.

There was considerable danger involved. The girls were often threatened. Leah and Katie did not seem to mind, but Margaretta and Mrs. Fox were in a nervous agony all the time.

In Albany, New York, an angry preacher swore out a complaint against them to the police. He accused Katie and Margaretta of blasphemy against the Holy Scriptures. The police refused to act against the girls, but a noisy mob broke up the séance. At this point Mrs. Fox, over the angry objections of Leah, decided that her daughters would be safer in New York City. Barnum had promised them full protection and fifty dollars a week for each girl. Since their expenses would be less, this would be more than they made in their private tour.

One of the things that helped Mrs. Fox make up her mind to join Barnum was the news that the great showman had signed Jenny Lind to appear under his management in the United States. Jenny, the "Swedish Nightingale," was

The Fox sisters about 1850, in a drawing based upon a Currier and Ives print. Margaretta, left, was close to fifteen. Katie, center, was about thirteen. Leah, right, was thirty-six.

one of the most famous opera singers of the day and certainly the most beautiful. She was giving up her opera career for the concert stage, since it promised more rewards. Mrs. Fox decided that if someone as famous as Jenny Lind could work for Barnum, then it would not be a disgrace for her daughters to appear for him.

However, she refused to let them appear at the American Museum with the freaks and the humbugs. Barnum agreed that he would set a room aside for them at his Barnum's Hotel. This was agreeable to Mrs. Fox and Leah. The girls went to New York in June 1850.

Miss Lind was not due to arrive until September. Barnum devoted all his time to the Fox sisters until the Swedish Nightingale arrived. His first publicity stunt in their behalf was to invite all newspaper editors in New York to come and receive a message from Spiritland via the Fox sisters' "spiritual telegraph."

Greeley was among the first. As it happened, his *Tribune* was the fairest of all the New York papers in its treatment of Katie and Margaretta. The famous editor wrote nothing himself about this first New York séance. He left the writing to George Ripley.

Ripley said the two girls sat quietly on a sofa in the parlor room of the hotel. Then near the close of the séance someone suggested that they move to a different part of the room. This was to prove that there was no mechanical rapper hidden in the sofa.

The girls agreed. Margaretta walked to one side of the large room. Katie went to the other side and stood by the door. Both girls were dressed in black silk and were very grave during the whole performance.

Raps sounded on the ceiling and wall around Margaretta. On the other side of the room louder knocks were heard on the door beside Katie. According to Greeley, Katie was then twelve years old. She was so small and slender that she looked younger. Her dress fell all the way to the floor like a woman's instead of to mid-calf, the length younger girls wore. If Leah and Mrs. Fox hoped to make her look older by dressing her as an adult, they failed completely. Despite her grave face, Ripley thought she was enjoying herself. Her eyes seemed to sparkle each time the ghost rapped near her. Once she laughed, which brought a stern look from Leah. Although Katie became plainer as she grew older, in her childhood she was the prettier of the two.

The editors and reporters moved over by Katie to listen to the rapping on the door.

Ripley reported that the sounds were heard on both sides of the door. "They produced a vibration on the panels that was felt by everyone who touched them. Different gentlemen stood on the outside and inside of the door at the same time. Loud knockings were heard on the side opposite to where they stood."

On the other side of the room where Margaretta stood, the same kind of rappings began on the door beside her. Ripley said that both girls were far enough from the doors so that it was impossible for them to have made the sounds.

The girls then went to another room on the next lower floor where they again produced the spirit rappings. This was to prove that the other room had not been set up to aid them in any way.

Ripley did not claim he had witnessed messages coming from the dead. But he did say: "Such are the most important facts as we recall them. We believe we have stated them without any coloring whatever, as they appeared to everyone present. But as to their origin or nature, we are as much in the dark as any of our readers."

The New York *Herald* took a different view. The angry editor wrote: "These blasphemous knockings should be put an end to, the parties arrested, and sent to the lunatic asylum. No respectable person, we trust, will countenance what is rank insult to God. The whole wretched mess will explode before long. Meanwhile, we caution people how they are gulled out of their money by the Rochester humbugs."

Another paper reported that a marching band passed in the street during the séance. "The spirit stopped the conversation and rapped in tune to the music until it was out of hearing." Was this just mischievous Katie Fox having a bit of fun?

Another reporter said, "I cannot tell how these knockings were made. It may have been by some machine concealed under the clothing of the girls. Perhaps their ankles or knees, pressed against the legs of the table, produced the knocks. . . . I think the girls made the knocks alternately, as one or the other was more closely watched. I do not believe they can persuade the spirits to make the raps in, or on, any place. Any one who is not willing to take my opinion of this, can see for himself or herself by calling at Barnum's Hotel, and paying the moderate price of one dollar for admission."

This writer's opinion was contradicted by a reporter from the New York *Express* who said, "Those who accuse the ladies of making the rappings, or of being a party to the mode of making them, will be satisfied in a short time that such is not the case. This is because the sounds were heard at so many different places at the same time and in different sounds. It would be impossible to produce them with any machinery."

He, like George Ripley from the *Tribune*, mentioned the sounds coming from both sides of the door. He added that when the knocks sounded near his foot he could feel the floor shake.

The stories aroused great interest in the girls. Barnum was delighted with business. The girls worked six hours a day. The first séance was held from ten in the morning until noon. Then after a two-hour rest, Katie and Margaretta received a new group at two, ending the second séance at four. In the evening they were back for another two-hour session from six until eight.

The Fox sisters remained with Barnum through September. After Jenny Lind arrived, Barnum devoted all his attention to her. He was paying the famed Swedish Nightingale one thousand dollars a concert. He felt he had to handle her publicity himself if he hoped to make back his money. Sometime before she gave her first concert on September 11, 1850, Barnum took Jenny to Horace Greeley's home where the Fox sisters were holding a private séance.

Earl Wesley Fornell, in his biography of Margaretta, claims that Jenny was jealous of the pretty Fox sister. This does not seem to have been the case. Jenny was a far more beautiful woman than either of the Fox sisters and much more famous. In fact, Miss Lind compared with any beauty of her time.

Also we have this newspaper story, which Emma Hardinge said was from the Cleveland *Plain Dealer*.

JENNY LIND AND THE SPIRITS

It is well known that Catherine Fox, a child of some twelve summers, is at present and has been for some time stopping in the family of Horace Greeley, in New York. When Jenny Lind learned of the marvelous things heard in the presence of Katy, as she is called, she went to Mr. Greeley's to see her.

It is said that the sweet songstress had a very interesting interview with what she believed to be the spirits of departed friends. When she left she kissed little Katy, saying, "If it were possible for you to make these sounds, I know it is impossible for you to answer the questions I have asked this evening."

Jenny had been talking in her native tongue [Swedish].

One of the most famous séances took place soon after the Fox family arrived in New York. It was a private affair at the home of Rufus Griswold, a noted editor and writer. George Ripley of the *Tribune* was there in place of Horace Greeley, who was busy. James Fenimore Cooper, William Cullen Bryant, and George Bancroft were also guests. Cooper was the distinguished author of *The Last of the Mohicans* and other famous novels. Bryant was the great poet who wrote "Thanatopsis" and other poems. Bancroft was a noted historian and former secretary of the navy.

Ripley's account of the evening tells how different guests

put questions to the spirits and were answered by the rappings. In the case of one questioner, the raps were so faint and run together that no sense could be made of them.

The poet and editor William Cullen Bryant asked no question, but was a sharp observer. Ripley wrote: "Mr. J. Fenimore Cooper was then asked to question the spirits. He proceeded to do so with the most imperturbable self-possession and deliberation." We can suppose that Ripley meant that Cooper kept a poker face.

Cooper chose his questions with great care. He wanted his questions to be a genuine test. He was determined not to ask any question at whose answer the girls could guess. Cooper's first questions likewise brought faint, hard-to-understand raps. The famous novelist then tried a different approach.

"I am thinking of a person. Is it a relative?" he asked.

The spirit rapped yes. There was no hesitation.

Cooper neither admitted nor denied the truth of the answer.

"Was this person a near relative?" he asked after a delay.

The answer was a quick yes. Cooper said, "A man?"

The spirit was silent. It remained so as Cooper asked if the person was a woman. There was an answering rap.

Cooper took quite a while before asking his next question. He looked thoughtfully at the two girls. They sat on a sofa across from the men. Katie and Margaretta sat together in the center. Mrs. Fox and Leah sat on each end of the sofa with a space between them and the girls. Margaretta dropped her eyes modestly when Cooper stared at her. Katie looked boldly back at him.

"Was this person I am thinking of my wife?" Cooper asked.

There was no answering rap. Cooper ignored Margaretta and looked straight at Katie as he asked if the person was his mother, a friend, or a sister. He got no answer until he said sister.

"When did this person die?" he asked.

The other men leaned forward expectantly. This was a trick question. Cooper had not said, nor had the question been asked before, if the person was dead or alive.

There were no answering raps. Then Leah said softly, "That is a question that cannot be answered yes or no by rapping. Can you ask it in a different way?"

Cooper nodded. "How many years has this person been dead—if the person really is dead?"

The raps started immediately and went on for a long time. Each person in the room except Katie and Margaretta kept count of the raps. Margaretta seemingly had lost interest. She stared at the wall. Katie, a half smile on her face, looked straight at Cooper.

When the rapping stopped, Cooper asked the others what number they got. One man said forty-five. Another counted fifty-four. Cooper did not say how many he had counted.

He asked the girls, "Can you ask the spirit to repeat the raps? Do it more slowly, so we can all get an accurate count."

"It isn't necessary to ask him," Katie said. "He heard you. He will do so if he wishes. We do not control him."

Cooper apologized, and the rappings began again. There

was a pause after each rap. When the spirit finished, all agreed that there had been fifty raps this time.

The novelist said nothing. His face was blank. One of the previous guests had exclaimed in surprise each time the spirit answered one of his questions correctly. Cooper kept such a bland expression that none of those present could tell if the spirit had correctly answered or had gotten any or all wrong.

Cooper was doing this deliberately. Someone had suggested that the girls could tell—like shrewd poker players —from a person's expression what answer to give. He did not intend for this to happen to him. He wanted a real test to see if a spirit was answering or if a couple of clever young ladies were tricking him.

George Ripley wrote: "Mr. C. now asked, 'Did she die of consumption?' He went on to name several diseases to which there was no answer. 'Did she die by an accident?' The answer was yes. 'Did she die by lightning? Was she shot? Was she lost at sea? Did she fall from a carriage? Was she thrown from a horse? Was—' "

Cooper was interrupted by a rap that meant yes. The famous novelist leaned back in his chair. He stared hard at the two girls. Then turning to the other men present, he said, "I have no further questions to ask of the spirit."

"The answers you received—?" Reverend Griswold asked.

Cooper did not immediately answer. Then he said slowly, "The person I inquired about was my sister. She died fifty years ago this week. She died from injuries received when—when she was thrown from a horse."

The Fox women, with the exception of Katie, sat quietly looking at the men. They gave no sign of satisfaction or happiness at being proven right. Katie had a half-smile on her face. It seemed to one of the men that she was trying to control a laugh.

There was a dead silence in the room after Cooper finished speaking. Then Griswold asked, "Did any of you gentlemen present know that Mr. Cooper had a sister who died fifty years ago after falling from a horse?"

None did. Then Griswold asked Cooper, "Do you think any of these ladies could have known of this before?"

Cooper shook his head. "I do not see how they could have known it," he said quietly.

James Fenimore Cooper was quite old at the time. He did not live long after this. Cooper's biographers do not mention it, but Spiritualist literature claims that just before he died the novelist told his nurse to "thank the Fox sisters for making it easy for me to go."

This endorsement from such a famous man greatly helped the Spiritualist cause. It was, Leah proclaimed, proof that "there is no death. In dying the spirit only moves from one plane of life to another in Spiritland."

After finishing their three months' contract with P. T. Barnum, Leah and Mrs. Fox decided not to renew it. Friends insisted that Barnum was such a "humbugger" that association with him made many people think the sisters were tricksters.

The girls gave a series of private séances in homes and were Horace Greeley's house guests for several days.

Greeley's New York *Tribune* carried a number of stories about the girls. They had all been written by George Ripley. When the Fox sisters and their mother left New York to return to Rochester, Greeley wrote the story himself, signing it with his initials.

Greeley's story said:

> Mrs. Fox and her three daughters left our city yesterday. They returned to Rochester after a stay of some weeks in New York. During this time they were subjected to every reasonable test. The rooms which they occupied at the hotel have been repeatedly searched. The girls have been taken without an hour's notice into houses where they had never before entered. Without knowing it, they were placed on glass surfaces hidden under the carpet.

Many people thought the Fox sisters were using electricity in some manner to make the raps. Glass is a nonconductor of electricity. The glass was placed under the carpet to cut off any secret electricity the investigators thought they might be using.

> The ladies have been disrobed by a committee of ladies. Such committees were appointed without notice. Neither of them could leave the room until the investigation had been made, etc, etc. Yet we believe at this moment no one pretends that he has detected either of the young ladies in producing or causing the "rappings." We devoted what time we could spare to this subject. It would be the basest cowardice not to say that we are convinced beyond a doubt of the ladies' honesty and good faith.
>
> Whatever may be the origin or cause of the "rappings," the ladies in whose presence they occur did not

make them. We tested this thoroughly, and to our entire satisfaction. The ladies' conduct and bearing are as unlike that of deceivers as possible. We think no one acquainted with them could believe them capable of engaging in anything so daring, impious, and shameful as this would be if they caused the sounds.

After leaving New York, the sisters split up. Mrs. Fox and Leah decided that each would take one of the younger girls. They would conduct séances in different places and take in twice as much money. Katie and Mrs. Fox remained in Rochester, putting on séances at Leah's home. Leah and Margaretta went to Albany and then to Buffalo.

Despite Greeley's kind words and the good showing they had made in New York, trouble was building up for them. One of the spearheads in this was C. Chauncey Burr. Burr was the hypnotist-lecturer whom Leah had refused to let attend a séance. The public interest in Spiritualism had reached such a peak that Burr decided he could make more money exposing the Fox sisters as fakes than he could with his old Bio-Electricity lectures.

Burr got his brother to help him. The two men pledged themselves to "destroy the Fox witch women!"

8

"Destroy the Witches!"

The Fox sisters first heard of Chauncey Burr's new attack on them from Horace Greeley. The editor sent Mrs. Fox a copy of a letter Burr wrote to the New York *Tribune*.

Mrs. Fox could not read. Katie read the letter to her. Burr claimed: "I have not only discovered how the rappings are done. But by much practice I found that I could do them myself. My raps are louder than those done by these mediums. They are done in a manner no person could detect, if I chose to impose upon them."

Many persons before Burr had claimed to know the secrets of the rappings. Spiritualists asked in return a question that exposers found hard to answer. This was how the girls could answer questions whose answers they could not have known without the help of spirits. Those asked by Fenimore Cooper were a favorite example that Spiritualists pointed to.

Burr tried to explain this as well. Burr said, "When I demonstrated that the raps could be produced by art, it still remained to be explained how the answers from the pretended spirits were, in many cases, so satisfactory and wonderful.

"This I have already explained in my lectures on Imagination and Ghost-Seeing. I have seen my brother, Heman Burr, do remarkable experiments with the mind. In these he produced more wonderful effects upon the imagination than any medium in a séance. In the short course of scientific lectures which I shall give at the Hope Chapel in New York on Monday evening, January 13th [1851], I shall not only show how rapping noises are made, but will also make plain how satisfactory answers are obtained from the 'spirit world.'

"I cannot fail to show any man, who is not already made crazy by the 'spirits,' that the whole mess of the 'knockings' is perfectly explained a good way this side of the other world!"

Leah showed the letter to Capron. He said, "This man is just trying to get publicity for his poor lectures. Spiritualism is true. There is nothing he can do to hurt it or you."

Capron talked about going to New York to hear Burr's lectures. But he could not get away from his work. "Anyway," he told Leah, "the newspapers will be full of it. Our friends in New York will send us copies of the stories. I don't think there will be any trouble exposing Burr's trickery for what it is."

Newspapers, for the most part, hailed Burr's coming lectures. One said, "At last this rapping humbug will be exposed!" Such free advertising caused the lecture hall to be jammed with people, including both believers and disbelievers.

Burr was a witty speaker. The audience cheered his thrusts at the Fox sisters and laughed at his jokes. As an ex-minister of the gospel, he liked to weave in biblical support for his arguments.

"Foxes are sly creatures!" he thundered. "But they cannot outfox an old foxhound! The Bible warns us to beware of foxes! Especially *little* foxes! In the Song of Solomon 5:15 are these words: '. . . the little foxes, that spoil the vines: for our vines have tender grapes.' Be likewise warned against our own *little Foxes*, for our bodies have tender souls! Be careful you do not sacrifice those tender souls to Satan, who works through witches disguised as mediums!"

The audience cheered as Burr denounced Spiritualism and the Fox sisters in particular. Spiritualists in the audience were dismayed at the reception.

Most of the New York newspapers hailed Burr's speeches, but Horace Greeley's *Tribune* was not one of them. George Ripley said that the raps Burr made in his demonstration sounded different from those that sounded in the *presence of* Katie and Margaretta. Ripley was careful not to claim that the two girls *made* the sounds.

"The sounds made by Burr were so far from being identical with the spirit rappings, that we are forced to the conclusion that they could not be made by the same means," Ripley said. "They were as different as the notes of a flute are from the notes of a trumpet."

Burr claimed that he made his raps by cracking the

joints of his toes. He said that he could make the audience think they came from different places merely by turning and looking at the places he wanted the people to believe they came from. This is a trick used by ventriloquists.

Ripley replied, "If Mr. Burr's sounds are produced by the toe joints, the Rochester sounds are produced in some other way. There was a peculiar ring to the Rochester rappings which Mr. Burr did not produce on this occasion."

As to Burr's claim that he made his audience think the sound came from different places just by turning his eyes to that point, Horace Greeley disagreed. He told of one séance with Katie where a two-year-old was present. The rappings seemed to be coming from a table set apart from Katie. The child walked over to the table and stared at the spot where the raps seemed to come from. Greeley claimed that the two-year-old's attention could not have been misdirected as an older person's might.

Burr had said that he would exactly reproduce the Rochester rappings. As Ripley pointed out, the sound of the raps was not the same. Spiritualists made much of this to prove that Burr had not exposed the Fox sisters at all. Capron told the girls not to worry.

"Burr has been discredited," he said. "No one important will believe him now."

But Burr was not defeated. He and his brother Heman insisted that all spirit mediums produced raps in *exactly the same way*. This was done by cracking the joints of the big toe. There were many reasons why the raps sounded different at different times, they said.

"These are the size and shape of the big toe, how tight

one's shoes are, the thickness of one's shoe soles, and what one is standing on," the Burr brothers claimed.

Chauncey Burr ended his lectures in New York and started a tour of major US cities with his exposé of the Fox sisters. Spiritualists followed him, giving the other side of the story. They repeated Ripley's claim that Burr's rappings did not sound like those genuine ones made in the presence of the Fox sisters. They also asked sarcastically if anyone thought that Katie's small toe could be cracked loud enough to be heard throughout a large auditorium.

Leah had been afraid that Burr's lectures would cause people to stop coming to hear Katie and Margaretta. Margaretta was tearful and wanted to quit. Leah became very angry with her. She demanded to know how Margaretta expected them to eat if they gave up holding séances.

Katie did not want to quit, but she often sided with Margaretta in these family arguments. Like Margaretta, Katie resented their older sister. Leah was bossy and strict. She considered herself responsible for the family's growing fortune. This was true. If Leah had not pushed her mother and sisters, the rappings in Hydesville would soon have been forgotten. Margaretta and Katie, of course, were the heart of the séances, but Leah's business operations made them profitable. She had no intention of stopping them now.

It was not an easy life for the young girls. Their childhood stopped when they became professional mediums. They spent six hours each day giving séances. Then sometimes they went out at night to give more at private residences.

Katie and Margaretta had practically no time for themselves. It was all work and no childhood play. There was no time for parties, games, or fun. The grim, determined figure of Leah Fox Fish was always there pushing the younger girls into more sittings for those who wanted to rap with ghosts. Both girls grew more and more bitter toward their domineering older sister. Mrs. Fox always sided with Leah. The girls' father, brother, and married sisters had no part in their lives. As a result, Katie and Margaretta grew closer to each other as they drew away from Leah and Mrs. Fox.

Once Katie, after a quarrel with Leah, cried fiercely, "When I am grown I'm going away and none of you will ever see me again!"

After Burr left New York, Leah had a long talk with Capron, Isaac and Amy Post, and George Willets about what she should do next. They all agreed that the girls should continue giving séances, but that the team should be broken up.

Capron said that Leah and Margaretta should keep touring upstate towns. "But it is important that séances be resumed in New York as soon as possible. This will show New Yorkers the big difference between Burr's fake toe-rapping and the real thing done by spirits," Capron said.

Leah wanted to go back to New York herself. Both Mr. and Mrs. Post and Capron said it would be better if Katie was the medium in New York.

"She is so small and young looking," Mrs. Post said, "no one could possibly believe she was making the raps like Burr said."

Leah agreed to this. She also agreed that Mrs. Fox should go with Katie. Katie, although the younger, gave Leah more trouble than Margaretta. Leah preferred to have Margaretta with her.

And so Katie and her mother went back to New York. Greeley welcomed them, but suggested that Katie and Margaretta should be educated. Mrs. Fox, illiterate herself, had a great respect for education. She agreed, but hesitated to take any action without talking to Leah. Also, there was the matter of how they would make money if both girls went to school. She told Greeley that she would agree to let one girl go if Leah agreed. Greeley said that he would pay for Katie's education.

Margaretta and Leah went to Albany and then to Buffalo, New York. Here they suddenly faced an attack on their honesty that was far more serious than Burr's.

Margaretta was holding séances in the Phelps House, a hotel in Buffalo. On February 15, 1851, a spiritualist friend came to see them. He was greatly concerned. He said that he was employed by the local newspaper, the Buffalo *Commercial Advertiser*. Three very famous doctors, who were also professors of medicine at Buffalo University, were going to expose Margaretta as a fraud. They had written a long letter to the newspaper which the man had seen. The letter was to be published shortly.

The men, all medical doctors, were Austin Flint, editor of the *Buffalo Medical Journal*, Charles A. Lee, Professor of Physiology, and C. A. Coventry, Professor of the Practice of Medicine. Leah's informant was so awed by these famous men that he was sure that they had solved the secret of the rappings. He advised Leah and Margaretta to leave town quickly. He was sure they would be arrested for fraud after the letter appeared in the paper.

Leah's eyes flashed. She drew herself up and said angrily that she would not be frightened into leaving.

"For three years liars have been threatening to expose us!" she cried. "Not one has succeeded yet. We have been investigated, cursed, threatened by mobs, stripped by vicious women, and insulted by disgraceful men. And what have they proven? Nothing! Let these great doctors do and say what they will. In the end they will make fools of themselves, just as that vicious man Burr has done."

Margaretta twisted her hands nervously. But she did not say anything. When Leah was in a rage like this, it only made her worse to argue with her.

There was nothing in the paper on either of the next two days. The Fox sisters decided that their friend had been mistaken, or that the newspaper had decided not to publish this new attack upon them.

Then on February 18, 1851, the letter appeared. A dozen people grabbed copies as soon as they came off the press. They rushed to the Phelps House to show them to the Fox sisters.

Leah refused to read the story. "I don't have to read it," she snapped. "It is nothing but another pack of lies. I wouldn't soil my eyes on cheap trash put out by misguided fools!"

However, she kept one of the copies. Later when she got rid of the crowd, she and Margaretta read it carefully in their room.

The letter read:

> To the Editor of the *Commercial Advertiser*:
> Curiosity led us to the Phelps House where two fe-
> males from Rochester (Mrs. Fish and Miss Fox) profess
> to talk with spirits. We have arrived at an explanation of
> these rappings, the correctness of which has been dem-
> onstrated. We felt that a public statement is called for.
> Perhaps this statement will prevent further waste of
> time, money, and credulity, to say nothing of sentiment
> and philosophy, in connection with this so long success-
> ful fraud.

In this letter the doctors said they investigated the same
way that they would diagnose a disease. This was to find
out first what it was *not*. The first thing they decided was
that the raps were not caused by spirits. They would not
even consider that the raps were made by ghosts until they
proved that they could not have been made by any human
being.

Next, they considered if the raps could have been caused
by something Margaretta or Leah (who sat next to her
during the séances) had hidden in her dress. This possibil-
ity was marked off their list "because it is understood that
the females have been repeatedly and carefully examined
by lady committees."

(This part of the letter put E. W. Capron in a rage. He
complained that the doctors called Margaretta and Leah
"females" instead of either ladies or women, while calling
the members of the searching committees "ladies." He
said this was insulting. One of the doctors retorted that he
saw no reason for calling two outrageous crooks "ladies.")

Next the doctors said the raps could not have been made by any mechanical device attached to tables, doors, or walls. The raps were heard in different parts of a room the girls had never been in before.

"So much for negative evidence," they wrote. "Now for what positively relates to the subject.

"On carefully observing the faces of the females, it was evident that the sounds were due to the younger sister," the doctors said. "She tried to conceal the fact that she was making an effort, but she did not succeed. We could see that she was making an effort, and she could not do this for long without getting tired."

The doctors said the next question they asked themselves was how could Margaretta make these rapping noises without movement of her body. The answer was, in their minds, by contracting muscles somewhere in her body.

The doctors then became somewhat technical in their explanation, using such difficult to understand terms as "the movable articulations of the skeleton." They meant the joints in which the bones of the body move due to the pull of various muscles.

The body joints are made with bones that end in knobs. These fit into sockets in the adjoining bone. The two are held together by cartilage—a tough, elastic gristle—and muscles. When a bone slips out of its joint, it is said to be "knocked out of place." This sometimes happens in body contact sports such as football and in different types of accidents.

Some people have such loose joints and cartilage that they can easily slip certain bones from their sockets. The doctors claimed that this is what Margaretta was doing.

She pushed the bone from its socket by tightening up certain muscles in her leg, they said. This would cause two knocking sounds. One when the bone snapped out of joint and a second when it snapped back into place.

"By a curious coincidence," the doctors reported, "after arriving at this conclusion, we discovered in Rochester a woman who can make precisely the spiritual rappings in this manner. She does this with her knee joints. The sounds are similar to those made by the Rochester impostors."

After giving a technical explanation of how the woman slipped her leg bone from its socket, the doctors said, "This is done without an obvious movement of her limb. It causes a loud noise."

"That is not true!" Margaretta said when the girls finished reading the letter.

Later Capron read it. "Fight them back!" Capron told the sisters. "Chauncey Burr is a fraud and everyone knows it. What he says will never hurt you. But these men are college professors. People will believe them because of what they are. For the sake of Spiritualism, you must fight and prove them wrong."

"I'm sick of all this fighting!" Margaretta cried. "I don't want to give any more séances."

Leah turned on her in a fury. Capron was embarrassed by the family quarrel. He left the room.

Leah wrote to her mother and Katie in New York. She enclosed a copy of the doctors' letter as it was published in the Buffalo newspaper. Katie had already seen it. Dr. Lee had written a summary of the letter and sent it to Horace Greeley.

Leah also sent Katie and her mother a copy of a letter she wrote to the newspaper about the doctors' charges. She said angrily, "We are not willing to rest under the charge of being impostors. We will undergo any proper and decent investigation."

Leah asked only that she be permitted to have six friends present at the investigation. This was to ensure that the doctors did not take advantage of her and Margaretta. She asked that such an investigation be made as soon as possible.

The doctors could not refuse. They had called Margaretta a faker without any real proof. They had gone to her séance as paying guests. They listened to the raps, and then, because they knew a woman who could crack her knee joints, they loudly claimed that Margaretta was doing the same thing.

This, everyone agreed, was not real proof. Therefore the doctors were forced to accept Leah's challenge and make a real investigation. They met to plan how they could "trap the Foxes."

·9·

The Fighting Foxes

Leah had cause to regret her haste in demanding that the three doctors examine Margaretta during a séance. In all the other challenges, the examiners had been baffled. They could find no way to explain the rappings. The doctors, however, had already decided how it was done. They set out to keep both Leah and Margaretta from using their feet in any way.

As doctors, the three men understood the muscles in the human body. They insisted that both Leah and Margaretta put their legs in such a position that all muscles in them would be tense. In this position the tense muscles would lock the joints in place. Or so the doctors thought. Their trick apparently worked for they waited a half hour and there were no spirit raps.

When they allowed Margaretta to put her feet normally on the floor light raps were heard. The doctors considered this proof of their claim that the spirit raps were made by Margaretta's knee joints.

In another experiment the doctors permitted Margaretta to sit normally. Then Dr. Lee placed his hand upon her knees to feel for any side movement if raps occurred.

Earlier, even quiet Quaker George Willets was ready to fight when the mob at Corinthian Hall wanted to inspect Katie and Margaretta's skirt hems. Ordinarily for a man to put his hand on a young girl's knees in public—or in private, for that matter—would have been outrageous. However, Lee was a medical doctor and therefore in a different class from ordinary men. In their report the doctors hastily pointed out that the pressure on Margaretta's knees was made through her dress.

This time there were knocks and Lee claimed to have felt a definite side movement of Margaretta's knee at the time. The doctors considered this proof of their theory.

In the report they wrote: "That sounds so loud could be made in this manner will probably surprise even medical people. Perhaps it will even seem incredible. In fact, after our explanation was first published some said it took almost as much stretch of the imagination to believe such sounds came from joints, as that they involved supernatural spirits."

Dr. Lee immediately left for New England. He found a man who could snap his joints. Joining with this loose-jointed man, Lee began giving lectures exposing the "Rochester impostors."

Back in Buffalo, Leah came out fighting. The *Commercial Advertiser*, the newspaper that first published the doctors' attack on the Fox sisters, invited Leah to defend herself.

She did not deny that the rappings were not heard when their legs were put in a strained position. "Our friendly spirits retired when they saw us put in such harsh proceeding by our persecutors," she claimed.

She attacked the way the investigation was handled. She contradicted Lee on many points. She also claimed that more friendly committees later used the same methods of the doctors, but found no evidence that the noise came from the medium's knees.

"Professor Lee, unlike the other doctors, came many times to listen to our regular séances. He heard spirit answers that were correct and astonishing. Yet he did not try to account for these answers."

Leah went on to say that she had feelings like other mortals. And her hurt feelings demanded justice.

Leah got what she considered justice, to the great surprise of the doctors. The publicity from the newspaper arguments between her and the Buffalo professors caused even more people to come to Margaretta's séances. These people wanted to believe in Spiritualism and it did not take much argument on Leah's part to convince them that the doctors were wrong.

Dr. Lee was the most disgusted of them all. He found that his lectures exposing Spiritualism were increasing the business of mediums wherever he went. He gave up and went home.

Leah was having trouble with Margaretta and she was ill. She was also nervous and exhausted from her fight with the doctors. This caused her to be more cross and demanding than usual. Margaretta finally rebelled. She told Leah she could not stand her any longer. She left for New York to join her mother and Katie.

She told her mother that she would never give another séance. However, she would listen to Katie when she would not pay any mind to Mrs. Fox and Leah. Within a few days Katie had Margaretta back with her at the séances.

Margaretta by this time had developed into a lovely girl. She put her hair up woman fashion, while Katie still wore long pigtails trimmed with black silk bows. Margaretta was about fifteen or sixteen. Already young men were turning to stare at her as she walked down the street.

Leah left Buffalo and went back to Rochester. She was sick in bed when a letter came from Cleveland. Chauncey Burr was to give a lecture there. Leah's friends wanted her to come and give a demonstration at the same time, thus proving Burr's claim wrong.

Leah refused. She said she was sick in bed, and that Katie and Margaretta were in New York with their mother. Other letters came pleading with her to come to Cleveland. Then a Spiritualist in Cleveland sent Leah a clipping from the Cleveland *Plain Dealer*.

This story disturbed her very much. She showed it to Capron and to Calvin Brown, the young man who had moved into their Rochester house after the mob attack following the Corinthian Hall meeting. It was thought best to have a man on the premises to protect the women. Brown, however, was very sickly. It is questionable how much help he could have given.

The *Plain Dealer* story, which had appeared in the May 7, 1851 issue of the newspaper, said, "The lectures given by Mr. Burr are both entertaining and convincing. Unbelievers will find reasons as plentiful as blackberries for thinking all mediums are impostors."

Capron pointed to this and told Leah that she had to go. "This man is hurting Spiritualism," he said. "If you don't go and prove him wrong, people will keep on believing him."

"But the newspaper is really on our side," Leah argued. "Look—here the editor calls the report of those Buffalo doctors a 'horse laugh.' "

"The people themselves—the ones we have to get on our side if Spiritualism is to grow as it must grow—are *believing* this man. You must prove to them that Burr is wrong."

"But Katie and Margaretta are in New York," Leah protested.

"Then you must do it yourself," Capron argued. "You are now a medium. You have been conducting séances right here in Rochester. You have done well at it."

"I can't do it!" Leah protested. "I'm sick. I just can't go."

But even as she spoke, she knew that she must go. It would be dangerous, for although she had given some séances on her own, she did not have confidence in herself as a medium. She was afraid that she could not make a good enough showing against Burr's showmanship.

But at the same time, as Capron and Brown pointed out to her, if she did not go it would look as if she were afraid of Burr. Spiritualists in Cleveland would lose faith in her.

Spiritualism had now become her life. Nothing else was as important to her. Life had been harsh from her childhood. Now for the first time Spiritualism gave her the money she had always lacked. It also gave her importance. While she was constantly threatened and called a fraud by many, still she was regarded almost as a high priestess by many others. Leah Fox Fish had tasted the sweetness of fame. She did not intend to give it up without a struggle.

Sick as she was, she was determined to go to Cleveland and fight Chauncey Burr the best she could. She could not go alone. Nice women did not travel alone in 1851. Leah got her sister, Maria Smith of Hydesville, to go with her. Calvin Brown also went along, and Mrs. Smith had to bring her infant son.

The party arrived in Cleveland on May 14. The editor of the *Plain Dealer* came to see her. He wrote: "Mrs. Fish seems an intelligent lady. She is agreeably spoken. A few minutes conversation in her plain, earnest manner removes the mystery which imagination has placed about her. You also forget the prejudice which slander may have attached to her character."

Leah was much better at explaining than she was at the séance table. She charmed the editor and then read to him a number of letters she had received from famous people.

Fortunately, Leah did not have to give any séances herself. On the day after her arrival in Cleveland, Katie and Margaretta arrived. The young girls were chaperoned by an older woman, Mrs. Mary Kedzie. Margaret Fox, who was getting old and ailing, did not feel able to make the trip herself.

Leah was surprised when the girls arrived. She had not asked for them because they were so busy in New York.

Katie claimed it was her idea to come. Mrs. Fox did not require much persuading. She too was worried about Leah trying to put on her own séance in Cleveland. She agreed for the girls to go, even though it would be costly. The séances in New York would have paid them twice what they could hope to get in Cleveland. But, like Leah, Mrs. Margaret Fox had gotten a taste of fame and money. She realized, as her older daughter did, that Chauncey Burr was becoming more dangerous to them. Too many people were beginning to believe what he told them about the Fox sisters.

Katie and Margaretta were not a part of their older sister's and their mother's financial scheming. Katie just enjoyed herself. Margaretta got fun out of the séances when she worked with her younger sister, but she hated it when she was with Leah.

The *Plain Dealer* reporter liked the young girls. He also noted that their rappings "were more than threefold louder than with Mrs. Fish alone." He thought this was because the girls' "spiritual batteries" were stronger.

He looked at Katie's impish eyes and pigtails, and into Margaretta's sweet face, and wrote: "No man of common sense can stand in their presence one moment without having all ideas of fakery knocked out of him.

"Mrs. Fish said that with these little girls, who are the most perfect known mediums, she would not fear to face all the skeptics in the world.

"The Fox sisters will remain at the Dunham House a few days. We would advise those hardshells, those mullets, who will not believe that one should rise from the dead, to go and take lessons from these little girls."

Leah was delighted to have her two sisters arrive, but her hunger for money soon got the better of her. They averaged from $50 to $100 a day—a remarkable sum for the time. Girls of Katie's and Margaretta's age were then working twelve hours a day in factories for as little as $3.50 a week. Even so, Leah saw no reason for wasting both girls on one séance. By splitting up, they could make twice as much.

So when a letter arrived from Spiritualists in Cincinnati inviting the Foxes to visit their city, Leah was delighted. She kept Margaretta with her in Cleveland because she could control Margaretta better than she could the more independent Katie. Katie, chaperoned by her sister Maria Smith and their friend Mary Kedzie, was sent to bring Spiritualism—the Fox brand—to the Ohio city.

As always, Katie was a personal hit. She had a knack of making everyone like her. Even Chauncey Burr, for all of his attacks on the Fox sisters, found Katie amusing. There is a story that Burr was standing at a curb in Cleveland waiting for some wagons to pass so he could cross the street. Suddenly he heard raps all around him. He looked up startled and saw Katie passing behind him. He laughed and she winked back at him.

She had always been called Katie, but the editor of the Cincinnati newspaper called her "Miss Catharine Fox." This delighted Katie, for it made her feel more grownup.

The story in the Cincinnati paper said that "Miss Catharine Fox, the spirit medium, accompanied by a married sister and a female friend, is in Cincinnati and will be pleased to meet those who desire to investigate spirit rapping." The writer then said that he had been present the night before at one of Katie's sittings. "The rappings we heard, to say the least, did not appear to be produced by any physical effort of the medium. Miss Catharine is a very interesting girl. She looks very far from being capable of carrying on any humbug whatsoever. We can do no less than request our readers to examine a séance for themselves."

Those who knew Katie best did not agree with the writer's statement about her being incapable of carrying on any humbug. They thought her, of all the Fox family, the most capable of humbugging.

Katie was in Cincinnati only a short time. Maria Smith's son became ill, and his mother took the infant back to Hydesville. Katie then returned to Cleveland to rejoin Leah and Margaretta.

The Hydesville ghost had long since been replaced by more famous spirits. A report of a séance conducted by Katie after her return to Cleveland said the rapper was Benjamin Franklin. Ben gave a rather sketchy talk—slowly spelled out by rappings—about the difference between matter and the spirit. As befitted one who made his scientific reputation by his studies of electricity, Franklin said, "Electricity and magnetism are always connected with matter, and belong to it." He claimed that clairvoyance—the ability to see the unseen world—was done by insulating one's mind from the material world. This permitted the medium's mind to make clear contact with the occult or spirit world.

A lot of people were outraged at the claim that Benjamin Franklin's ghost would waste time rapping with Katie

Fox. But Spiritualists found nothing incredible about it. They claimed Franklin would have been just the person to work for a way to communicate between the living and the dead.

This is undoubtedly true. Franklin would have been interested. As a result Ben became a popular guest with a number of mediums. In one case Franklin was reported as saying that a group of scientific minds in Spiritland worked out the means for spirits to act upon the magnetic force of mediums and so to communicate with the earth. He did not say why, with all the scientific minds of the ages to work with, they permitted a murdered man (identified later as Charles Rosna) to succeed in making the first contact with the living.

After business fell off in Cleveland, Leah and the two girls went to Cincinnati to finish the work Katie had begun there. Two newspapers got into a public argument over the girls. Both admitted "that Burr's and the Buffalo doctors' claims are the silliest humbug theories." But one editor insisted that the girls had some mechanical rapper hidden in their clothing. The women who searched them had been too stupid to find it, he said.

Shortly after they arrived in Cincinnati, Calvin Brown became deathly sick. Doctors told Leah that he would not live. She and Calvin had been talking of marriage for some time. Now at the young man's urgent request, Leah agreed to the marriage. A minister was summoned and they were married in Brown's bedroom. Calvin lay in bed. Leah stood beside the bed, holding Calvin's hand. Katie and Margaretta were witnesses.

Calvin Brown had never believed much in spirits. And the spirits had shown their annoyance when he moved into the Fish home by playing tricks upon him. Now that he was soon to join them, the spirits seemed to have forgiven Calvin. As the minister read the marriage ceremony, the spirits gently rapped a chorus to his words.

After the ceremony Katie said to Margaretta, "Wasn't that nice of the spirits?"

Margaretta smiled and agreed that it was.

Leah remained in Cincinnati to talk to a lawyer about filing a libel suit against Chauncey Burr for calling them fakes and impostors. Katie and Margaretta took Calvin back to Hydesville where David Fox's wife helped nurse him.

Burr was not the least bit bothered by the threatened lawsuit. He had just made a discovery that he thought would "finally trap those sly Foxes!" Although Burr professed to have an admiration for Katie, his new attack centered directly around her.

When the storm broke, the Fox sisters were dismayed, for this was the most damaging attack they had yet faced.

·10·

The False Friend

In the past Chauncey Burr had sent all his letters to the New York *Tribune*. This time he skipped Horace Greeley's newspaper. His new letter charging the Fox sisters with fraud was sent to the New York *Express*. This paper was an enemy of Spiritualism. Burr expected his story to get a bigger play there.

Burr was a chubby man, bald-headed and with the mobile face of an actor. He looked grave and angry when he denounced the sisters. He looked sly as he cracked his toe joints to show how he thought Katie and Margaretta made their raps. Now he was jubilant as he said that he had at last "trapped the Foxes."

"Sly as they are," he cried, "there is no way they can slip out of this trap. I have proof, gentlemen, proof!"

Leah and Mrs. Fox were told of Burr's new attack. Neither was concerned. They had grown used to their enemy's attacks, none of which had hurt them.

But they were shocked when the story appeared. Burr had gotten Mrs. Ruth Culver to sign a statement which was witnessed by a doctor and a minister. Mrs. Culver was the wife of Mrs. David Fox's brother. While not a blood relative, she was a member of the inner family circle. So when she accused Katie and Margaretta of fraud, readers thought they were getting inside information. This hurt more than the charges of the Buffalo doctors or Burr by himself.

Mrs. Culver swore that Katie and Margaretta spent a lot of time at her house. "For two years I was a sincere believer in the rappings," she said. Then during a visit to Leah's home in Rochester, Mrs. Culver saw some things that made her doubt that real spirits were at work.

Mrs. Culver did not say what it was that aroused her suspicions. But it is quite possible that she did see something. In the beginning Spiritualism consisted only in conversing with the dead by means of spiritual rappings. Then as this began to pall on the public, the hundreds of mediums who followed Katie and Margaretta began to expand their ghostly activities. Glowing figures were seen in the dark. Ghostly hands materialized. Spirit music was played. And other strange things happened.

In later years Margaretta told a friend, "All Spiritualism is a fake except the rappings." Yet, to keep up with the public interest, the Fox sisters also added these new developments to their séances. This included spirit writing. In spirit writing the medium goes into a trance while holding a pencil in her hand. Then the medium's ghostly control takes over, guiding the medium's hand in rapid writing. The writing is always backward and must be read held up to a mirror. The writing is then assumed to be a message from the spirit world.

If we assume that the rappings were genuine spirit messages, we still must admit that the Fox sisters added—to keep up with the competition—some tricks.

Also, all mediums experienced times when their powers deserted them. In such times they often resorted to trickery to carry them over until they could again make contact with their spirit controls. The great Cheiro—a noted medium and palmist of the early twentieth century—had this experience. D. D. Home, most famous of mediums, often lost contact with his spirit friends. After an unfortunate experience when he tried to fake a contact, he just announced that "the power has left me" and retired from mediumship until his power returned.

In the light of such experiences, it is possible that Mrs. Culver did see something in the Rochester house that aroused her suspicions.

On the other hand, this guess must be balanced against some things that were revealed about Mrs. Culver at a later time. Mrs. Culver, it appears, was jealous of the large sums the Fox sisters were earning. She thought she should get some of it, and suggested to Leah that she should be employed to chaperone the girls and assist in the séances.

Leah, with her hunger for money, was not about to share with anyone unless she absolutely had to do so. She very sharply turned Mrs. Culver down. Then later Mrs. Culver had a quarrel with David Fox and his wife. Spiritualists said that this proves that Mrs. Culver was just out for revenge. Also, there was profit involved as well, for Burr paid her to make her written statement.

According to Frank Podmore (in *Modern Spiritualism*),

Margaretta admitted to Mrs. Culver that the rappings were fakes. The woman then approached Katie and offered to help make raps at the séances.

Mrs. Culver's statement does not mention Margaretta. The woman said a cousin of hers from Michigan wanted to ask the spirit some questions.

> I told Catharine that I should be able to answer nearly all the questions my cousin would ask. I said I would do it if she would show me how to make the raps. She said that, as Margaretta was absent, she needed somebody to help her. She said that if I would become a medium, she would explain it all to me.
>
> Catherine said that when my cousin consulted the spirit, I must sit next to her, and touch her arm when the right letter was called. I did so, and was able to answer nearly all the questions correctly.
>
> After I had helped her a few times in this way, she revealed to me the secret of the rapping. The raps were produced with the toes. All the toes were used. After nearly a week's practice, with Catharine showing me how, I could produce the raps perfectly myself. At first it was very hard work. Catharine told me to warm my feet, or put them in warm water. Then it would be easier to rap, she said. She claimed she had to warm her feet three or four times in the course of an evening. I found that heating my feet did help me to rap easier.

Mrs. Culver claimed that Katie told her how to guess the correct answers. One wonders why, if the young medium could do this, she had to get Mrs. Culver to help her answer the cousin's questions.

Catharine said it was generally easy enough to give the right answers if the one who asked the questions called the alphabet. She said she and Margaretta liked to have the questioner write down several names on a piece of paper and then point to each one until the "spirit" rapped yes. She said this gave them a chance to watch the faces and motions of the persons. In this way they could nearly always guess correctly. Catharine also told me how they moved tables.

At this point in the story, Burr added a note saying, "Mrs. Culver gave us some illustrations of this trick." The newspaper story did not explain how this was done. However, causing a table to rise and even to rap out messages itself is a common medium's trick. In the case of one fake medium, the trick was done in this manner:

The medium had a metal band around his forearm, hidden under his sleeve. A flat metal bar was attached to this. It extended just to the edge of the medium's cuff. It could not be seen. Then when the medium placed his fingertips on top of the table, the bar slipped unseen *under* the edge of the table. He then only had to raise his arm in order to raise the table.

Catharine told me that all I should have to do to make the raps heard on the table would be to put my foot against the bottom of the table when I rapped. If I wished to make the raps sound distant on the wall, I must make the raps louder, and direct my eyes earnestly to the spot where I wished them to be heard.

She said if I could put my foot against the bottom of the door, the raps would be heard on the top of the door.

Catharine also told me that, when the committee held their ankles in Rochester, the Dutch servant girl rapped with her knuckles under the floor from the cellar. The servant was instructed to rap whenever she heard their voices calling the spirits. When I was in Rochester last January, Margaretta told me that when people insisted on seeing her feet and toes, she could produce a few raps with her knees and ankles. . . .

The whole secret was revealed to me with the understanding that I should act as a medium when the girls were away. Catharine said that whenever I practiced, I had better have my little girl at the table with me. People would not suspect so young a child of any trick.

When Catharine was instructing me how to be a medium, she told me how frightened they used to get in New York for fear somebody would detect them. She gave me the whole history of the tricks they played upon people there.

The *Express* published the story with great glee. The editor pointed out that his newspaper had always maintained that fraud and dishonesty were back of the rappings. "Now," he said with great satisfaction, "we have a full admission, from the lips of persons who acted as confederates of the Fox girls, that the whole affair was, as the *Express* said it was, an imposture of the most dishonest character."

Leah, for once, kept quiet. E. W. Capron, the Foxes' old friend, leaped to their defense. He claimed that Katie denied talking to Mrs. Culver about rappings. He revealed the quarrel between Mrs. Culver and the rest of the Fox family. Next, he pointed out that the Fox family had never employed a "Dutch servant girl." Also, that the investigations where Mrs. Culver said the Dutch girl rapped on the cellar floor were not held in any place that had a cellar. They were held in various offices selected by the different committees and on the stage of the Corinthian Hall.

Capron challenged Burr to deny that this was a lie. Burr could only say that perhaps there was another investigation witnessed by Mrs. Culver that he and Capron did not know about. Spiritualists hooted at this lame explanation by Burr and repeated it widely as proof that Mrs. Culver's statements were a pack of lies.

Capron also asked how vibrations were felt on doors and walls if the Fox sisters were only snapping their toe joints and making listeners think the noise came from the walls simply because the girls stared at the walls.

Capron did his work well. The public in general refused to believe that two young girls could fool so many famous people. The publicity, instead of destroying the Fox sisters, as Burr hoped, brought new crowds to see them wherever they went.

Spiritualism in general continued to grow. The number of mediums increased. With the increase came continual exposure of fraud and trickery. A particularly horrible example came to light in October 1851. A thirteen-year-old girl named Almira Bezeley had become a rapping medium earlier in the year. Like the Fox sisters earlier, she was tested repeatedly without anyone's discovering any connection between her and the raps.

In the course of a séance held in the summer, a spirit said that the Bezeleys' infant son would die in the fall. The child did die in October. This was first hailed as proof of Spiritualism. Then some suspicious actions by Almira caused the local sheriff to question her rather harshly. The girl broke down and confessed that she had killed her brother in order to make the spirit's prediction come true.

Many times unbelievers tried to get the police to put a stop to Spiritualism. They seldom succeeded. Unless actual fraud was discovered that in some way injured someone, the police could not act. If a spirit advised a widow to entrust her savings to a medium who then stole the money, the police could act. But in séances where nothing illegal happened, it was not a police matter—as one chief put it —"to step in just because idiots made fools of themselves."

Angry unbelievers did succeed in bringing an eighteen-year-old girl medium to trial. This was on a charge of disturbing a church service. The girl was named Abby Warner. Abby was an orphan. In addition she was crippled and ugly. A widow named Mrs. Kellogg, who lived in Massillon, Ohio, felt pity for Abby and took her in as a servant. Here it was discovered that Abby was a powerful spirit medium.

Emma Hardinge says of Abby, "She had lived under such neglect and ignorance that she could read only printed characters imperfectly. She could neither write herself nor read writing. Yet, in a state of deep trance, this uneducated girl would write correctly with both hands, at the same time, on different subjects with different spirits."

While writing two messages, one with each hand, at the same time, Abby could also converse with still a third spirit through raps.

This was such an extraordinary achievement that many thought that ugly Abby was in league with the devil. No normal person could possibly write different messages at the same time with her right and left hand, and spell out still another with her voice.

Abby fell ill and had to have an operation. This had to be a charity treatment, for Mrs. Kellogg could not pay for it and Abby was a pauper. It never occurred either to her or to Mrs. Kellogg to charge for the séances the girl gave.

The doctor employed by the poorhouse officials to give Abby her needed operation was convinced that the girl was a fraud. He could find nothing to prove it and fell back on Burr's charges against Katie and Margaretta Fox. The doctor wrote to a Cleveland paper claiming Abby was using her toe and knee joints and the muscles of her chest to make the raps.

This came to the attention of Dr. Abel Underhill (who may have been related to Daniel Underhill, Leah's third and last husband). Dr. Underhill was a Spiritualist. He took Abby into his home for treatment during the remainder of his visit to Massillon.

On Christmas Eve, 1851, Dr. Underhill took Abby to Saint Timothy's Episcopal Church for the evening services. After Abby was seated, loud raps broke out in the auditorium. The angry rector demanded that the rapping stop. It ceased for a short time and then started again. It continued during the services and kept time to the songs.

The next day an angry member of the church swore out a complaint against Abby. There was a law against creating a disturbance in a church.

The Cleveland *Plain Dealer* reported: "As this is the first modern instance in which 'the spirits' have been brought to a court of justice, a report of the trial will doubtless be interesting to the public at large.

"The trial commenced on December 27 [Saturday] before R. H. Folger, Justice of the Peace. A. C. Wales appeared for the State [that is, he was the prosecuting attorney], and Messrs. Keith, Underhill, and Pease, for the defendant."

Witnesses described the noise in church. Two men said they went down in the church basement to see if the noise came from there. It appeared to them as if it came from the floor where Abby was sitting. Another witness said that Dr. Underhill was known to be a Spiritualist. This was, he said, a plot of these Spiritualists to disturb a Christian meeting.

"Abby's counsel admitted that the sounds were heard, but denied that she caused them. No witness was found who could swear to seeing the slightest movement in the Spiritualist party. On the contrary, those who had watched the 'spirit rapper' closely were forced to admit that not even her dress moved, during the time when the raps were loudest.

"Two ladies who sat in the same pew with Abby were against Spiritualism. Yet they admitted that she never moved during the knocking. They never suspected her of making them. Indeed, they seemed to think that the sounds came from a more distant point.

"Others said the raps came from the back, side, ground, or at any rate, distant from Abby. They all strangely disagreed on the exact direction."

The trial continued for three days. At the end, Justice Folger ruled, "It is to be regretted that the true source of this disturbance cannot be found, and the offender punished. A church has been disturbed. But after three days' investigation, the guilty party is undiscovered. The investigation has been fruitless. The court can only express its sincere regret. Being unable, in the light of the proof, to find the defendant guilty, she is discharged."

Justice, in regard to the occult, had come a long way since the days of the Salem witch trials, when an accusation meant death.

The Fox sisters were not involved in this famous trial, but Leah turned it to her advantage. It proved, she said, that rappings were not made by mediums.

Whenever she got a chance Leah liked to point out: "Spiritualism is true. It has been *proven* in court!"

However, her troubles were not over. In time she would face the most damaging enemy of them all. This enemy, strangely enough, was her own sister, Margaretta.

· 11 ·

Hero of the Ice Land

Leah Fox Fish Brown may have thought that a court decision would convince people that mediums really were "spiritual telegraphs," but the people quickly showed that they did not want courts mixed up in Spiritualism.

The Honorable John W. Edmonds of the New York Supreme Court had been a very highly regarded judge. He had also been a very interested observer of the Fox sisters during their New York séances. Later Justice Edmonds talked at great length about Spiritualism with Horace Greeley and others.

Edmonds' wife had died not long before this, and he grieved deeply for her. He was thus eager for any proof that Spiritualism could put one in contact with his beloved dead. The judge became a very ardent Spiritualist. His young daughter Laura showed talent as a rapper, and conducted séances for her father.

The judge made no secret of his beliefs. Spiritualists spread word about him even farther. They considered it good for Spiritualism to have such a famous man among their followers.

The general public took an opposing view. Justice Edmonds was accused of consulting the spirits about his court decisions. He soon found himself in the center of a public storm with angry demands for his resignation from the bench.

In a very reasonable reply that he sent to the papers, Judge Edmonds said his position entitled people to question his judgment, but not to question his religion. He considered Spiritualism as part of the religion he believed in.

"One writer," he said, "with a want of feeling, speaks of my 'consulting my dead wife' in making my decisions. Another says that it is 'rumored' that I have consulted spirits in regard to my court decisions. Another says that my belief is 'opposite to all divine revelations,' and that it is fit 'for no other system than devil worship.' Still another said that my beliefs are a surrender of judgment.

"All these statements are wide of the truth. I might complain that I am attacked because I hold beliefs unpopular to part of the community. But I did not sit down to write for the purpose of complaining. I know that it is not so much me as it is the faith which I profess, that is the object of attack."

Judge Edmonds went on to explain that he had not wanted to visit the "Rochester Rappers," but a friend insisted. He admitted that Katie and Margaretta surprised him. He went back to see them several times with the intent to expose their fakery. Instead he became a convert. He insisted that too many people condemned them without actually observing Katie and Margaretta working with the spirits.

"I was at a loss," he said, "to tell how the mediums could cause what I witnessed. The mediums walked the length of a suite of parlors, forty or fifty feet. The rappings were heard distinctly five or six feet behind them, the whole distance, back and forth, several times. Near the top of a mahogany door, higher than the girl could reach, I heard sounds as if the door was struck by a hard fist."

He also spoke of table tippings and furniture being moved without anyone near it. He mentioned people being pulled by strong unseen forces.

He said that having seen so many strange things at séances he carefully read all "explanations" that appeared in newspapers. "I could not but smile at the rashness and futility of the explanations," the judge said. He included the Buffalo doctors and their claim that Margaretta made the raps with her kneecaps.

After defending himself, Judge Edmonds resigned from the court. He entered private law practice, but kept up his Spiritualist work. He did not, however, associate again with the Fox sisters. He and George T. Dexter formed their own spirit circle. Edmonds' daughter Laura and Dr. Dexter's daughters, aged nine and fourteen, acted as their mediums. Later the two men wrote a well-known book about Spiritualism.

Once the judge had resigned, newspapers that had attacked him praised his ability as a justice. The *Evening Mirror* in New York said, "Whatever may be his faults, no one can justly accuse him of a lack of ability, industry, honesty, or fearlessness."

Judge Edmonds, it should be stated, is no relation to the author of this book.

Other people in public and in business also found that being known as Spiritualists hurt them. In one town two mediums were mobbed, covered with tar and feathers, and driven out of town for being "devil worshipers." In New York a spirit circle was exposed as a "love cult" engaged in supposedly "wicked actions." The writings of the famous Andrew Jackson Davis were held up as proof that Spiritualists were godless men.

All this controversy disturbed Margaretta Fox. She had been unhappy with her life as a medium for some time. At the same time her feelings toward her domineering sister Leah grew more bitter. She again said she wanted to quit, but her mother refused to let her. Mrs. Fox had agreed to let Horace Greeley send Katie to school. Margaretta was needed to support her family. While Leah stayed in New York with Katie, Mrs. Fox took Margaretta to Philadelphia to hold séances there.

They arrived in Philadelphia in the fall of 1853. Later Margaretta said she was fourteen years old at the time. Others have given her age as sixteen. In any event, she created a sensation. Webb's Union Hotel gave her the bridal suite for her séances and all agreed that she was lovely.

A newspaper described her at this time: "She is a very interesting and lovely young lady, and is very young. She has large dark Madonna eyes, a sweet expressive mouth, a petite and delicately molded form, and a regal carriage of the head, with an aristocratic air quite uncommon."

Among those who came to hear the rappings were the grown daughters of a famous Philadelphia family, the Kanes. The girls talked so much about the rappings when they got home that they excited the interest of their famous brother, Elisha Kent Kane.

Kane was then thirty-one, and one of the most famous men in America. He had been sickly as a child, but fought to overcome this. In his teens he became an explorer and then studied medicine. His father's influence got him appointed an assistant surgeon in the US Navy when Kane was only twenty-two.

In 1845 the famous British Arctic explorer Sir John Franklin set out to find the Northwest Passage—a water route around the top of Canada from the Atlantic to the Pacific oceans. He was lost and several expeditions set out to find him. When the British rescue ships failed to find Franklin, Henry Grinnell, a New York merchant, financed a ship to hunt for the lost explorer. Kane was taken along as ship's doctor. They sailed in 1850, but returned the following year without finding any trace of the lost ships.

Grinnell did not have enough money to finance another ship completely, and Kane began giving lectures on the Arctic to raise the extra money. It was understood that he would be given command of the Second Grinnell Expedition, as it came to be called.

It was at this point that the Arctic hero—and Kane's work on the first expedition entitled him to be called a hero—went to the Union Hotel to hear the famous "Rochester Rapper."

Kane was directed upstairs to the bridal suite. When he walked in, the first thing he saw was Margaretta. She was seated by the window, studying her French lesson. He stopped and stared at her. The light from the window made a halo around her hair.

Margaretta Fox, about the time she met Elisha Kane.

"I must have made a mistake," Kane said to Mrs. Fox, who came up to him. "I was seeking the 'Rochester Rapper.'"

Margaret Fox smiled. She was used to people who thought the séances were held in dark, mysterious places. "No," she said. "You are in the right place. That is my daughter Margaretta, the medium."

Margaretta had given the handsome visitor a hasty glance while he talked with her mother. Then she turned her eyes back to her book and acted as if she did not know he was there until Mrs. Fox called to her.

Kane paid more attention to Margaretta than he did to the famous rappings. He came back the next day and the day after that. Soon he was calling twice a day. After Margaretta and Mrs. Fox returned to New York, Kane found that his fund-raising business needed him in that city.

Kane's interest in Margaretta was so open that New York newspapers began to print gossip about the two. Horace Greeley was angered and wrote a note in the *Tribune* saying this was a private matter between Margaretta and the famous "hero of the iceland."

The publicity angered Mrs. Fox, who told Kane he should not see Margaretta anymore. Kane insisted that he wanted to marry the girl. But he admitted that his aristocratic family would never accept "an unlettered girl." He was due to leave soon for his next trip to the Arctic. He asked that he be permitted to put Margaretta in a finishing school near Philadelphia while he was gone. They would be married upon his return.

Katie, who had been sent to school by Greeley, had found school boring and was back at the séance tables. Margaretta had come to the point where she hated the work so much that it was difficult for the family to keep her at it. So Mrs. Fox reluctantly gave permission for Margaretta to give up Spiritualism and learn to be a lady.

Leah was outraged and argued violently with her mother. Margaretta cried and Mrs. Fox sided with her unhappy daughter. Margaretta was enrolled in the fashionable Mrs. Turner's School for Young Ladies in Crookville, near Philadelphia. Shortly after, in May 1853, Kane sailed for the Arctic in his second attempt to find the lost British explorer, Sir John Franklin.

Kane was to be gone two years. During this time Margaretta developed such "mental disquiet" that she had to be taken back to New York to be with her mother. She gave a few séances and then went back to the school "because this is what Dr. Kane wants."

Another time she ran away from the school and joined Katie in séances in New York. But again she went back to school. Then when the two years had passed, there was no word of Kane's expedition. It was feared that its members, like the British explorers they sought, had vanished in the Arctic.

But Kane was not dead. He had taken his boat farther north than any person had previously gone. He discovered much new land, but finally his ship was locked in the ice. They ran out of food. Kane abandoned his ship and led his men in a perilous 1,300-mile hike across frozen water and ice-locked land to a Danish settlement in Greenland. They had traveled overland for ten months, arriving in August 1855. Kane finally reached New York in September 1855.

There was a tremendous celebration to welcome the returning hero. Margaretta was not part of it. She returned to New York to be there when Kane arrived, but he did not come to see her. He sent a friend to tell her that his family objected to his seeing her. Later he came to see her in secrecy several times. Then he left for England to see Lady Franklin, wife of the lost explorer.

Although no one knew it then, Franklin was dead. One wonders why Margaretta, with her ability to talk to spirits, could not have summoned this Franklin's spirit as easily as she had done Benjamin Franklin's. It would have saved fruitless rescue attempts, for the ghost of John Franklin could have told Kane that he and all his crew had been dead for five years.

Kane became ill in London and went to Cuba to regain his health. He died there on February 16, 1857. Margaretta collapsed with grief. Leah, whose husband Calvin Brown had died, tried to get the girl to join her in séances. Margaretta refused. Dr. Kane had wanted her to give up Spiritualism, and she would not offend his memory.

She began calling herself Margaretta Fox-Kane, claiming she and Dr. Kane had been married in a Quaker ceremony. This type of marriage only requires the couple to announce their intention before witnesses.

According to Margaretta's story, Kane had come to see her. Then "Miss Katharine Fox came into the room. Dr. Kane desired her to call her mother, who came upstairs to the parlor. . . . Dr. Kane informed them he had sent for them to witness the solemn declaration that would follow.

"Then standing up, and holding Margaretta's hand, while his left hand encircled her form, he said: 'Maggie is my wife, and I am her husband. Wherever we are, she is mine and I am hers. Do you understand and consent to this, Maggie?' Margaretta answered that she did."

This quotation is from *The Love-Life of Dr. Kane*, a book of letters Kane wrote to Margaretta. Margaretta had the letters published when the outraged Kane family demanded that she stop calling herself "Mrs. Fox-Kane."

It was said that Margaretta never had a happy hour from that time until the day she died. She lived with her mother and father in New York. John Fox, too old to farm anymore, had moved to the city. Leah married Daniel Underhill, a wealthy businessman, in 1858 and retired as a medium. However, she did support the cause and apparently was hoping to start a new Spiritualist religion with herself as its head. Katie was the only one who continued to give séances. The money she made went to support her parents and sister.

During the Civil War (1861–1865) Margaretta occasionally gave séances. Her heart was not in it and she did no more than just enough to earn a living. Several times Leah's husband had to help her financially. Leah claimed this happened off and on for five years.

John Fox died on January 19, 1865. Margaret Fox followed him to the grave in August of the same year. More than seventeen years had passed since the family first heard the rappings of the Hydesville ghost. Katie was now a woman of twenty-eight. Margaretta was about thirty or so. Neither liked Leah, although Katie's feeling against their sister was not as deep as Margaretta's.

After the war each sister went her own way. Margaretta returned to Spiritualism to support herself. Leah lived the life of a rich woman as Daniel Underhill's wife. Katie went to England in 1871. There, in December 1872, she married the British lawyer and Spiritualist Henry Jencken. The next ten years were the only really happy years of Katie's life.

She had two sons. When her husband died in 1885, Katie brought her children to the United States. For a short time she and Margaretta again gave séances together. Then a friend paid Margaretta's passage to England and the sisters were parted again.

While Margaretta was in London, Leah charged that

Katie Fox at about age thirty-five.

Katie was not a fit mother. She asked the Society for Prevention of Cruelty to Children to take the boys from Katie.

The charge was untrue. The boys were returned to their mother. Just what Leah had in mind in making such an accusation is not clear. She had grown to hate her younger sisters, but it seems that she wanted the boys given to her. There had been much in the newspapers about the boys being "baby mediums" when they were small. Perhaps Leah hoped to use the children as she had used Katie and Margaretta so many years before.

Margaretta returned to the United States as soon as she heard about Leah's charges against Katie. Margaretta was in a fury. She had always resented her older sister who had pushed her so hard during the early years of Spiritualism. This deep dislike had turned to savage hatred when Leah tried to prevent Mrs. Fox from letting Dr. Kane put Margaretta in the Philadelphia finishing school. Katie was the only person other than Kane whom Margaretta had ever loved. Now Leah's attack on Katie put Margaretta in such fury that at times she was not rational. She would walk the floor, tearing her clothing and screaming curses upon Leah.

This unhappy situation set the stage for an explosion that would rock the foundations of Spiritualism.

·12·

The Shocking Confession

piritualism is a curse!"

Spiritualists were stunned to read this statement by Margaretta Fox-Kane in a newspaper story. "The vilest people make use of spiritualism to cloak their evil doing," she said. "People like old Judge Edmonds and Mr. Seybert of Philadelphia become crazed. At the direction of fake 'mediums' such people part with their wealth as well as their common sense."

Margaretta helped found Spiritualism. It was unthinkable that she should turn against it now. Spiritualists were quick to point out that she was merely condemning crooked mediums. They were a "curse," but honest ones were not.

Margaretta soon showed that she was condemning *all* Spiritualism. She gave an interview after she arrived back in the United States. This one left no question about what she thought, or claimed to think.

The reporter, however, said that Margaretta acted strangely during the interview. Her voice rose sharply as she talked. Once she jumped up and danced around the room. Then she went over and started hammering on the piano. Loud raps broke out all around the room. Margaretta laughed shrilly at the raps. She cried, "See how easy it is to fool a newspaper man?"

Spiritualists refused to believe her story. After all, they had been hearing exposés of Spiritualism for forty years—it was then 1888. None of the previous exposés had hurt Spiritualism. This too, they thought, would be forgotten. However, Margaretta said she would repeat in a public forum all the things she had said to the reporter. She arranged a meeting in the Academy of Music hall in New York. The place was packed that evening.

Margaretta came on stage dressed in black. At first she was so nervous she could not talk. Then raps sounded on the stage around her. They seemed to give her courage to go ahead. She claimed that she made the raps by cracking the joints of her big toe.

Her voice trembled and became shrill as she cried, "Many here will scorn me. But if they knew the sorrow of my life they would pity me. When I began this fraud I was too young to know right from wrong. I hope God Almighty will forgive me and those who are silly enough to believe in Spiritualism."

A newspaper reported: "At this point Mrs. Kane became excited. She clapped her hands and danced about, crying, 'It is a fraud! Spiritualism is a fraud from beginning to end! It is all a trick. There is no truth in it.'"

Katie Fox Jencken was in the audience, listening to her sister. A number of different reports have been written about Katie's actions that night. One said she applauded loudly. Another had her on stage with Margaretta. Another said she rose in the audience and branded Spiritualism as a fake herself. The truth seems to be that she just listened quietly, saying nothing. Most agree that she was in sympathy with Margaretta.

Yet, the next day she wrote a letter to a friend. In it she said she had no idea that Margaretta would expose Spiritualism until she read the newspaper story just before the Academy meeting. She definitely disagreed in the letter with Margaretta's claim that raps were made with the toes. Katie said, "I could make a lot of money going on the stage and proving that the raps are *not* made in this manner."

In a newspaper interview, Margaretta gave her story of how the Hydesville rappings began. Her story—as we shall see—is not entirely true. Margaretta said:

"My sister Katie and myself were very young children when this horrible thing began. I was eight, and just a year and a half older than she. We were very mischievous children. We wanted to terrify our mother, who was a good woman but easily frightened.

"At night when we went to bed, we used to tie an apple on a string and bump the apple against the floor. Mother listened to this noise. She could not understand it, but did not suspect us of a trick because we were so young.

"At last she called the neighbors and told them about it. It was this that set us to learning a way to make the raps. It was a very wonderful thing that children should make such a discovery. Children will always find a means to make mischief. As to the thought of spirits, it never entered our minds. We were too young to know anything about that.

"My oldest sister, Mrs. Underhill, came to Hydesville

when the tricks first began. My sister, now Mrs. Daniel Underhill—she was Mrs. Fish then—began to form a society of Spiritualism."

She went on to tell how Leah took them to Rochester where Katie discovered how to crack their joints to make the raps. "It is astonishing how easy it is done," Margaretta said. "It is the result of perfect control of the muscles of the leg below the knee. These muscles control the tendons of the foot. They allow actions of the toe and ankle bones that are not commonly known."

She claimed the control necessary to make the rappings is possible only if one begins training at an early age. "A child at twelve is almost too old," she said.

"I am the widow of Dr. Kane," she told the readers. "I hold his memory dear. I would call him to me were it possible. I know there is no such thing as the departed returning to this life. I have tried to do so in every form. I know that it cannot be done."

She told how she had gone to a graveyard at midnight while in London. She went alone to each grave and stood over it, calling to the dead to speak to her.

"All was silent," she said. "I found that the dead could not return. There is no test left that I have not thoroughly sifted."

She then went back to talk of her unhappy childhood again. She told how Leah arranged their séances. "We had crowds coming to see us," she said. "Mrs. Underhill made as much as $50 to $100 a night. She pocketed this."

The farther she went into her story the more rambling her account became. At one point she claimed that Spiritualists thought her crazy, and certainly some of her actions and the way she talked indicated that her mind might be slipping.

One of the strongest things on her mind was her hatred of Leah Fox Fish Brown Underhill. She kept coming back to this time and again. At one point she said, "We were entirely under the influence of Mrs. Underhill during this dreadful time." Later she said, "Time and again I have told my sister, Mrs. Underhill: 'Now that you are rich, why don't you save your soul?' At my words she would fly into a rage. She wanted to start a new religion. She told me that she received messages from spirits. She knew we were tricking people, but she tried to make us believe that spirits exist. . . . I wish to say clearly that I owe all my misfortune to that woman, my sister, Mrs. Underhill."

After her sensational appearance at the New York Academy of Music, Margaretta went on a lecture tour. She drew poor crowds and her manager deserted her in Philadelphia. She claimed she received none of the money.

Shortly after this, Katie—doing poorly at regular séances—began her own lectures exposing Spiritualism. Her actions were extremely curious, leading to rumors that she—like some claimed of Margaretta—also was losing her mind. She would give lectures at night exposing Spiritualism, and during the day she would conduct séances for anyone who wanted them.

A reporter for a Rochester paper commented on her odd actions. He said that her manager kept a close watch on her, and that he had trouble getting an interview.

> She spoke in a parrotlike way. She said the same thing over and over, seeming to have learned it by heart. She

gave an explanation that didn't explain the way she made the rappings.

Her appearance in the theater was an utter failure. She was so nervous she could hardly sit still. She talked brokenly of the terrible mental strain she was under. Her words were delivered like a memorized lesson. Her explanation of the way she produced the rappings was childish.

The reporter's conclusion was that Kate Fox believed in Spiritualism and in her own powers as firmly as ever she had, but that in her weakened mind she had taken this way of getting money, possibly bread, for herself and her children. Her appearance did not, in this writer's mind, prove or disprove the truth about Spiritualism.

Spiritualists struggled to find proof that people talked with the dead before the Fox sisters started the rapping craze. They insisted that it was not important if the sisters were frauds. So were many others who had been exposed, but this did not lessen the fact that there were true mediums.

Others refused to believe that they were fakes. In a recent book on Spiritualism they were still being defended. This book said: "Years of public misunderstanding, the hostile atmosphere, and the drain on their nervous energy from too many sittings, and the complete absence of understanding as regards to the religious implications of Spiritualism served to undermine their senses."

The claim was made that the girls were alcoholic and did not understand their so-called confessions. Others claimed they had denounced Spiritualism out of fear of being killed by Spiritualism's enemies. And so the argument went on.

When they could not make a living exposing Spiritualism, both Katie and Margaretta returned to giving séances. Both women were now old and nervous. They lacked the ability to answer questions correctly as they once had done. The number who came to them dropped and both now lived in poverty.

Then on November 20, 1889, Margaretta declared that she had lied in denouncing Spiritualism. "Would to God," she cried, "that I could undo the injustice I did the cause of Spiritualism. I was under the strong mental influence of persons who hated it. They made me say things that were not true."

She said that she was speaking now because the spirits forced her to make a denial.

"At the time I spoke against Spiritualism I was in great need of money. Persons I prefer not to name took advantage of this. The excitement also helped upset my mind."

A reporter asked if there was any truth in the first story she told.

"It was all false," Margaretta insisted. "My belief in Spiritualism has not changed. When I said those dreadful things I was not responsible for my words. I challenge anyone to make the 'rap' under the same conditions which I will. There is not a human being on earth who can produce the 'raps' in the same way as they are through me!"

One wonders what Katie Fox thought about this last statement.

Margaretta's return to Spiritualism was a great relief to Leah. Mrs. Underhill, hearing that her sister was going to make her first confession, fled from New York. She went to Hydesville and stayed with her brother David until the excitement blew over. Margaretta's public outcry against her and the deep hatred of the younger woman were heavy blows to Mrs. Underhill. She withdrew into gloomy silence until her death in 1890. Neither Katie nor Margaretta went to their sister's funeral.

Katie, her mind becoming more and more unsettled, continued to hold séances. Then on July 2, 1892, her youngest son, Ferdinand, came home to find his mother lying on the floor dead of a heart attack. Friends tried to find Margaretta, but she had disappeared. Friends arranged for Katie's burial in a Brooklyn cemetery. Newspapers said she was fifty-six years old. If this was true, then she would have been twelve on that long ago day when she started modern Spiritualism by clapping her hands and crying, "Mr. Splitfoot! Do as I do!"

In February 1893 Margaretta was found unconscious in a shabby apartment. She was taken in by a friend, Mrs. Emily Ruggles, who got a woman doctor whose last name was Mellen to look after Margaretta. The unhappy woman was too far gone to save. She died on March 8, 1893.

In 1905, Dr. Mellen—who was not a Spiritualist—told the Medico-Legal Society of New York about Margaretta's last hours. After Margaretta regained consciousness there were loud raps in the room. When Dr. Mellen inquired about them, Margaretta whispered in a weak voice, "It is my friends watching over me."

Dr. Mellen claimed that Margaretta was then paralyzed and could not move hand or foot. On other visits the doctor similarly heard raps on the ceiling, on the floor, and on the walls. These came in response to whispered questions from the dying woman. Margaretta weakly explained to the doctor that her "friends" were preparing a place for her.

Were They or Weren't They?

The statements of the newspaper reporter who interviewed Katie and the doctor who watched Margaretta die show that both Fox sisters died believing that they could really talk with spirits.

This does not necessarily prove that they did. There is considerable evidence that both women's minds were failing at the last. What they thought then may not have been what they thought in their early years. Therefore a serious investigator, not concerned with the right or wrong of Spiritualism, cannot really say if Margaretta and Katie's earlier confessions of fraud were sincere.

One thing is certain. Margaretta's claim that she made raps sound on the ceiling, in doors, and around the room just by snapping the joint of her big toe and looking in a certain direction is not true. Neither they nor anyone else can make a table vibrate by cracking a joint. Yet we have the testimony of numerous people, including Horace Greeley, that they felt heavy vibrations. Margaretta may have been a fraud, but she did not tell the truth about how she made those raps.

Her confession included many other incorrect statements. She said they made the first raps by bumping an apple on the floor and that they did not learn to crack their joints *until they got to Rochester*. Actually, the girls were in the room with their parents and later in a room with all the neighbors when they conversed with the Hydesville ghost. They could not possibly have bumped an apple on the floor without being seen. Then rappings occurred on the boat going to Rochester. Where could they have bounced an apple in it? Margaretta said when they couldn't bounce the stringed apple, they beat on the bedstead. With the room filled with doubters could they have done this without being caught?

It is also important to remember that the newspaper reporter who interviewed Katie when she was exposing Spiritualism said that her explanation of the rapping was "childish."

In addition, the loose-joint theory was brought up and rejected many times by various enemies of the Fox sisters. Greeley and others said it just could not be done in this manner.

This is not said to argue that the Fox sisters were genuine mediums. But it is to argue that neither woman in her confession ever revealed the real truth about how the raps were made. They merely repeated the ideas first advanced by Burr. They kept the real secrets to themselves.

In another part of her confession, Margaretta said, "We never thought of spirits. This never entered our minds. We were too young." On the contrary, it was Katie who first asked her mother if the noise was made by a ghost.

Also, Margaretta was not all that young. She was at least twelve years old, instead of the eight she later claimed.

And so on with other various inaccuracies.

There have been various arguments to support the theory that the Fox sisters were true mediums in their youth, but lost the power as they grew older. This happened to Cheiro and the famous Daniel Dunglas Home, among others. Cheiro turned to trickery and Home retired at the age of thirty-five. The argument here is that it is extremely difficult to bridge the gulf between the world of the living and the world of the dead. Only certain gifted people have the "power," body electricity, or whatever one chooses to call it, to act as a battery for spirits to communicate. This gift gradually dies as one ages.

Those who knew or met the Fox sisters in the final days of their unhappy lives agree that both women seemed to believe sincerely in Spiritualism. Believers use this as proof that Katie and Margaretta were true mediums. Disbelievers claim that by this time they were half crazy and lived in a dream world of fantasy.

The evidence—looked at honestly—will support both views.

The strongest argument in the women's favor was their truly amazing ability to answer questions whose answers they could not possibly have known in advance. Katie's identification of James Fenimore Cooper's sister, dead for fifty years, is an example. This happened so many times that the answers could not have been accidental guesses.

However, they had this ability only in their younger days. They lost it as they got old.

We are told that they did this by studying the faces of their sitters. Mrs. Culver claimed that Katie admitted this to her. Many fortune tellers today use this trick. Poker players watch their opponents for nervous gestures that will give away the fact that the others are holding good hands.

It is admitted that this can be done in many cases. Surprise, shock, or disbelief on a sitter's face permits a fake medium to modify and expand on an answer to provide correct answers. But those who admit this ask, "Could a twelve-year-old girl do this?"

We have written reports of but one séance in which Katie Fox did this in the presence of people who were aware of this fortune-teller's trick. This was the séance attended by William Cullen Bryant, George Ripley, Rufus Griswold, General Lyman, James Fenimore Cooper, and other noted people of the day.

Cooper in particular tried to control his expressions and not let the medium know if an answer was true or false. Cooper and Katie were closely watched by distinguished men who should have noticed if Cooper's actions were giving Katie clues.

Was she tipped off in advance on what to answer? Not a person in the room knew of Cooper's long dead sister. Even if Katie had been told, she would not have known when the questioning began that it was the dead child—gone for fifty years—that Cooper had in mind.

Some have claimed that the girls were telepaths. They could read minds. Another theory was that they could generate "body electricity." This was released in pulses to create knocks around the room. Others who refused to believe in Spiritualism claimed there was some other occult explanation for the raps. Horace Greeley leaned in this way. He never believed in Spiritualism, but he still insisted that the girls were not fakes.

And so, no one can really say whether or not Katie and Margaretta Fox *at one time in their lives* could really talk to ghosts. But it must be admitted that, whatever they became in their old age, the Fox sisters were amazing little girls and young women. This is true whether they were true mediums, telepaths, "psychic batteries," explorers of a new occult science, or just plain tricksters.

Afterword

When a writer retells a story that is 130 years old, as this one is, the reader has a right to ask, "How true is this story?"

All the incidents of major importance noted here can be documented by more than one source. Documentation means that at one time or another somebody wrote or said that this is what happened.

Whether or not these newspaper reporters, letter writers, book authors, and other sources were right or not is something we must take on faith. By comparing what different people, friends and foes of Spiritualism said, we hope to get as close to the truth as possible.

Often accounts differed greatly. Sometimes the difference was minor. For example, when Katie first spoke to the ghost in the Hydesville house, her mother—in a signed statement—said that Katie's words were: "Mr. Splitfoot! Do as I do." Another writer said the words were: "Old Splitfoot! Do as I do." That is close enough. I chose to use Mrs. Fox's words, for she was there.

Sometimes I found it necessary to use material for which I could find only a single source. The letter of Katie Fox saying she could prove that Margaretta did not use her toe in making the raps is an example. I found this letter in Conan Doyle's history. There is no reason to doubt she wrote it. I just like to have more than one source when I can get it.

Most conversation in histories is re-created. Not even the person himself can recall *exactly* what he said at a given time. However, I used direct quotations from letters, articles, and accounts when I could. In some cases the quotations I used from these have been heavily edited. This was done to simplify them. Writers 130 years ago wrote rambling sentences that sometimes were strung out for an entire paragraph. They are difficult for modern readers to follow. So I often broke them into shorter sentences, eliminated unnecessary words, and sometimes substituted simpler words. I always tried not to alter the original meaning. My sole purpose was to make the material easier to read.

Here is an example, in which I was presumptuous enough to think I could improve upon the clarity of the famous journalist Horace Greeley. Greeley wrote:

> Mrs. Fox and her three daughters left our city yesterday, on their return to Rochester, after a stay here of some weeks; during which they have subjected the mysterious influence by which they seem to be accompanied to every reasonable test and to the keen analytical scrutiny of hundreds who have chosen to visit them, or whom they have been invited to visit.

Periods must have been in short supply in 1850, or else Horace disliked them. I used this extra-long sentence in this manner:

> Mrs. Fox and her three daughters left our city yesterday. They returned to Rochester after a stay of some weeks in New York. During this time they were subjected to every reasonable test.

In a similar manner other quotes were sometimes shortened.

A lot has been written about the Fox sisters. Most modern books that I have seen merely repeat what was said about the girls during their lifetime. For this reason, I relied most on the oldest books I could find. Of these, the most valuable were their friend Eliab Capron's *Modern Spiritualism: Its Facts and Fanaticisms* (1855), Emma Hardinge's *Modern American Spiritualism* (1870), and Frank Podmore's *Modern Spiritualism* (1902).

Capron is valuable because he was there almost from the beginning. He wrote of what he saw. However, he was an ardent Spiritualist and a friend of the Foxes. This has to be considered in believing what he wrote. He did include a lot of statements and newspaper articles that we can obtain from no other sources.

Emma Hardinge's book is also loaded with newspaper quotations and letters that give a variety of opinions and facts. Mrs. Hardinge's book is hard to read. References to the Fox sisters are scattered all through it. But since Emma published her book at her own expense, she did not include an index. One has to dig for information in her pages.

Frank Podmore wrote much on Spiritualism. He did not believe in it himself, but was remarkably fair in spite of that.

In this book I have dealt mostly with the youth of the Fox sisters. The trials of their later life have just been sketched in to make their story complete. There is much more to be said of their remarkable lives. Readers who would like to know more of this bitter period will find themselves searching through many dull and hard-to-obtain books. However, here is a short list of some more easily obtained books that might be an aid in further study:

Andreae, Christine, *Seances and Spiritualists*. Philadelphia: J. B. Lippincott, 1974.
> This book was written for young people and is easy to read. It has only a brief sketch of the Fox sisters. However, it gives a very good review of Spiritualism right down to modern times and serves as an excellent background for understanding this strange belief.

Capron, Eliab W., *Modern Spiritualism: Its Facts and Fanaticisms*. New York: Partridge and Brittan, 1855.
> An excellent source book by a man who was there.

Doyle, Arthur Conan, *The History of Spiritualism*. New York: George H. Doran, 1926.
> This book, in two volumes, by the distinguished author of the Sherlock Holmes stories, is easy to read. However, Doyle was an ardent Spiritualist and very gullible. He once accepted as true some fake fairy pictures that were so badly done even Spiritualists were embarrassed for him.

Edmonds, John Worth, and Dexter, George T., *Spiritualism*. New York: Partridge and Brittan, 1853.

As a judge who was forced to resign for his belief in Spiritualism, Edmonds may be called its first martyr.

Fornell, Earl Wesley, *The Unhappy Medium*. Austin: University of Texas Press, 1964.

This claims to be a biography of Margaretta Fox (called Margaret herein). However, it is really a history of Spiritualism in this period with a sketchy account of Margaretta's life woven through it. It is a scholarly type of book with many footnotes listing sources. The author practically ignores Katie and in some cases has credited Margaretta with things that Katie did.

Hardinge, Emma, *Modern American Spiritualism*. New York: Privately printed, 1870.

Somewhat difficult to read, rambling and poorly organized, but extremely valuable for any student of early Spiritualism. Mrs. Hardinge was quite a character and medium in her own right. She learned mediumship from the Fox sisters.

Kane, E. T., and Fox, Margaretta, *The Love-Life of Dr. Kane*. New York: Carleton, 1866.

This book, published by Margaretta to prove her marriage to Dr. Kane, is mainly letters that he wrote to her. The introduction gives some details of the Fox sisters' life and something about the background of the Fox family.

Kendall, Lace (pseud.), *Elisha Kent Kane: Arctic Challenger*. Philadelphia: Macrae Smith, 1963.

A young people's biography of the famous man who played such a vital part in Margaretta's life. Kane was a genuine hero.

Jackson, Herbert G., Jr., *The Spirit Rappers*. New York: Doubleday, 1972.
A good adult biography of the Fox sisters, but lacking in some material that seems to support the sisters.

There are literally hundreds of other books and publications that make reference to the famous sisters. Any interested person can find a lengthy bibliography in Fornell.

Although many of the books listed above are very old, they do not appear difficult to obtain. I found every one listed, except Capron, in the Los Angeles Public Library.

Index